MARION SHAW and SABINE VANACKER

REFLECTING ON
MISS MARPLE

ROUTLEDGE

LONDON AND NEW YORK

First published in 1991
by Routledge
11 New Fetter Lane, London EC4P 4EE

Simultaneously published in the USA and Canada
by Routledge
a division of Routledge, Chapman and Hall Inc.
29 West 35th Street, New York, NY 10001

Typeset by LaserScript, Mitcham, Surrey.
Printed in Great Britain by Cox & Wyman Ltd, Reading

British Library Cataloguing in Publication Data
Shaw, Marion
Reflecting on Miss Marple. – (Heroines?).
1. Fiction in English. Christie, Agatha, 1890–1976
Characters
I. Title II. Vanacker, Sabine III. Series
823.912

Library of Congress Cataloging in Publication Data
Shaw, Marion
Reflecting on Miss Marple/Marion Shaw and Sabine Vanacker.
p. cm. – (Heroines?)
Includes bibliographical references.
1. Christie, Agatha, 1890–1976 – Characters – Jane Marple.
2. Feminism and literature – Great Britain – History – 20th century.
3. Detective and mystery stories, English – History and criticism.
4. Marple, Jane (Fictitious character) 5. Women detectives in
literature. 6. Heroines in literature. I. Vanacker, Sabine.
II. Title. III. Series.
PR6005.H66Z88 1991
823'.912 – dc20   90-24121
                                   CIP

ISBN 0-415-01794-7

Violence, murder and a sweet, white-haired old lady are an unlikely combination. Yet, in her Miss Marple novels, this is exactly the combination which proved so successful for Agatha Christie. Why is this apparent contradiction so potent a formula?

Reflecting on Miss Marple explores the elements of the heroine's character which make her subversive, showing at the same time how she upholds the status quo. The authors place Miss Marple firmly in context as the quintessential post-war spinster. Marginalised by society and despised or trivialized by men, Miss Marple emerges as a feminist, triumphantly able to exploit contemporary prejudices against unmarried women in order to solve her case.

Marion Shaw and Sabine Vanacker examine the inherent contradictions of the Miss Marple novels, their social context, and their place in detective fiction as a whole. *Reflecting on Miss Marple* is an astute and engaging account of detective fiction and feminism which will attract readers from literary studies, cultural and media studies, and women's studies, as well as the general reader.

HEROINES?

Certain fictional women have become part of western mythology. They are the stars of novels, films, radio and TV programmes, which have caught the imagination of generations of women. What is the secret of their magnetism?

This new feminist series about literary heroines investigates their lasting appeal. Each writer explores her chosen heroine's relationships with other characters in the novel, with her own author, with readers past and present, and lastly with herself. These characters all touch chords of reality for us. By their very 'ordinariness' they demonstrate that, in the most general feminist sense, all women are heroines.

For general readers as well as students, these concise, elegantly written books will delight all lovers – and even haters – of the original classics.

Titles in the series include:

CONTENTS

IMPORTANT NOTE

Agatha Christie Ltd. expressly forbids the use of any material in a publication that would reveal the identity of the murderers in the Christie novels and, furthermore, makes it quite clear that such identification would invite legal action on their part.

In the interests, solely, of pragmatism therefore, we have made every effort to avoid 'naming names' even though we feel sure that the vast majority of readers of this book will be more than familiar with the Christie novels.

We invite our readers, like good detectives, to draw their own conclusions...

MS, SV

ABBREVIATIONS OF TITLES OF AGATHA CHRISTIE'S WORKS

Auto	*Agatha Christie: An Autobiography* (1977, London: Collins.)
ABH	*At Bertram's Hotel*
ACP	*The Adventure of the Christmas Pudding*
BL	*The Body in the Library*
CM	*A Caribbean Mystery*
FFFP	*4.50 from Paddington*
MCFSS	*The Mirror Crack'd from Side to Side*
MIA	*A Murder is Announced*
MMFC	*Miss Marple's Final Cases*
MF	*The Moving Finger*
MRA	*The Murder of Roger Ackroyd*
MV	*The Murder at the Vicarage*
PFR	*A Pocketful of Rye*
N	*Nemesis*
SM	*Sleeping Murder*
TDIWM	*They Do it with Mirrors*
TP	*The Thirteen Problems*
'TNC'	'The Tuesday Night Club', in *TP*

AGATHA CHRISTIE:
SOME BIOGRAPHICAL NOTES

1890 Agatha Mary Clarissa Miller was born in Torquay, Devon, on 15 September; the third child of Clarissa Margaret Boechmer and of Frederick Alva Miller, an American living mainly in England on an income stemming from the family business. Unlike her brother and sister, Agatha's education was largely informal, but included dancing, singing, and piano lessons. In her autobiography, she lovingly dwelt on a childhood which was very happy, even after her father died in 1901 leaving a difficult financial situation.

1906 Agatha Miller attended Miss Dryden's school in Paris, where she studied singing and the piano, and acquired the French which would prove so useful for devising Poirot's gallicisms.

1910 Agatha Miller enjoyed her coming-out season, in Cairo because of financial problems.

1914 Agatha married Captain Archibald Christie by special licence on Christmas Eve. During the Great War, she nursed in a Torquay hospital, and later worked in the hospital dispensary. She trained for the Apothecaries' exam, acquiring a close familiarity with drugs and poisons.

1919 Her daughter, Rosalind, was born in Torquay.

1920 Agatha Christie published the first of more than seventy detective novels. *The Mysterious Affair at Styles* featured Hercule Poirot and was published by The Bodley Head.

1922 *The Secret Adversary*, her second, less successful novel, introduced two other series detectives, Tuppence and Tommy Beresford. It was also the first novel to be filmed, by Fred Sauer in 1928, in *Die Abenteuer G.m.b.H.*

1923 Archie and Agatha Christie joined Major Belcher on a round-the-world trip, the British Empire Exhibition Mission, taking in South Africa, Australia, New Zealand, Fiji, Hawaii and Canada.

1926 Agatha Christie caused a minor literary storm over her treatment of the murderer in *The Murder of Roger Ackroyd*, one of her best Poirot novels, also the first book with a new, lifelong publisher, Collins.

Following the death of her mother and the initiation of divorce proceedings by her husband, Agatha Christie disappeared on 3 December. After a much-publicized search across four counties, she was rediscovered in a Harrogate Hotel, apparently suffering from amnesia, while living under the name of Teresa Neele, in part the name of the young woman Archie Christie wanted to marry.

1928 Agatha Christie and Colonel Archie Christie were divorced.

1929 Agatha Christie travelled through Turkey to Baghdad on the Orient Express. On a second visit, in 1930, she met the archaeologist Max Mallowan, Leonard Woolley's assistant at the Ur excavations.

1930 At the beginning of one of Christie's most productive decades, Miss Marple appeared for the first time as the village sleuth in *The Murder at the Vicarage*.

Christie had her first play, *Black Coffee*, performed at the Embassy Theatre and later at the St Martin's Theatre.

Giant's Bread was published, the first of Christie's non-detective, 'straight' and often autobiographical novels, published under the pseudonym Mary Westmacott.

1931 *The Sittaford Mystery* appeared with a non-series detective, Emily Trefusis, one of her best, strongly-plotted novels.

1932 Miss Marple was an armchair solver of puzzles, as put to a group of friends, the Tuesday Night Club in *The Thirteen Problems*. Some of these stories had already appeared before the first full-length Marple novel.

1934 *Murder on the Orient Express* appeared, later to be filmed to great acclaim by EMI in 1974, with Albert Finney as Poirot.

Another highly autobiographical novel, *Unfinished Portrait*, was published by Mary Westmacott.

1937 *Death on the Nile* appeared, it was filmed, again by EMI, in 1978, with Peter Ustinov as Poirot.

1939 *Ten Little Niggers*, or in the American edition, *And Then There Were None*, was published, one of Christie's best and darkest novels. During the Second World War, Christie again worked as a dispenser's assistant and continued to publish.

1942 After an interval of ten years, a third Marple novel appeared, *The Body in the Library*.

1943 Another Marple novel, *The Moving Finger*, was published.

1944 Mary Westmacott published *Absent in the Spring*, a novel charting the self-exploration of a middle-aged woman travelling in the Middle East.

1947 *The Rose and the Yew Tree*, another Westmacott novel, appeared.

1949 *The Murder at the Vicarage* was dramatized by Moie Charles and Barbara Toy and staged in London at the Playhouse.

1950 *A Murder is Announced* was published, with Miss Marple investigating a suspicious death during a murder game.

1952 A play, *The Mousetrap*, opened in London at the Ambassadors Theatre on 25 November, with Richard Attenborough, produced by Peter Saunders and directed by Peter Coates. Originally based on a radio play, *The Mousetrap* is still running in London.

They Do it with Mirrors: Miss Marple solved a murder in a school for young delinquents but discovered it was, as usual, a family affair.

1953 *A Pocketful of Rye*; the murder of her maid sent Miss Marple into another murder plot governed by the rules of a nursery rhyme.

1955 Agatha Christie Ltd. was founded, to deal with her many publications.

1956 She became a Commander of the Order of the British Empire in the New Year's honours list.

The last of the Westmacott novels appeared, *The Burden.*

1957 *4.50 from Paddington*; Miss Marple and her assistant Lucy Eylesbarrow detected the murder of a woman witnessed from an adjoining train by Miss Marple's friend, Mrs McGillicuddy.

Agatha Christie became president of the Detection Club.

1961 Margaret Rutherford created the role of Miss Marple in a Metro-Goldwyn-Mayer film, *Murder, She Said*, based on *4.50 from Paddington.*

Exeter University awarded Agatha Christie the degree of Honorary Doctor of Letters.

1962 *The Mirror Crack'd from Side to Side*; a filmstar and her entourage settled in St Mary Mead. When a guest at her reception was murdered, the event was witnessed by yet another hapless friend of Miss Marple, Mrs Bantry.

1963 *Murder at the Gallop* was another Rutherford film, this time however, based upon what was originally a Poirot story, *After the Funeral.*

1964 Miss Marple travelled to the West Indies and investigated *A Caribbean Mystery*.

Murder Most Foul and *Murder Ahoy! Murder Ahoy!* were the final Rutherford films, the latter with an original script by David Pursall and Jack Seddon. Its sole remaining connection with Agatha Christie was the figure of Miss Marple.

1965 Miss Marple distinguished illusion from fact when staying *At Bertram's Hotel.*

1971 Agatha Christie received the order of Dame of the British Empire.

Nemesis, in a sense a sequel to *A Caribbean Mystery,* had Miss Marple joining a tour of Famous Houses and Gardens of Great Britain in order to correct a miscarriage of justice.

1975 Agatha Christie's last Poirot novel, *Curtain: Hercule Poirot's Last Case* was published, with a final surprising murderer . . .

1976 Agatha Christie died on 12 January and was buried on 16 January in St Mary's churchyard in Cholsey, Oxfordshire.

Sleeping Murder: Miss Marple's Last Case was published posthumously, although it had been written during the 1940s.

Murder at the Vicarage was brought to the stage at the Savoy Theatre in London.

1977 Twenty-fifth anniversary of *The Mousetrap.*

A Murder is Announced was produced at the Vaudeville Theatre in London, opening on 21 September, in a scenario adapted by Leslie Darbon, with Dulcie Gray as Miss Marple.

An Autobiography was published, a loving portrait of her family and childhood and her later life with Mallowan.

1979 *Miss Marple's Final Cases,* a collection of short stories, was published.

1980 Angela Lansbury starred in *The Mirror Crack'd,* produced by the EMI team.

1983 *A Caribbean Mystery* was adapted for television by CBS Television, with Helen Hayes as Miss Marple. This was followed up by *Murder with Mirrors* in 1985.

1984 *Miss Marple: The Body in the Library* was adapted as a three-part television series by T.R. Bowen, with Joan Hickson starring as Miss Marple in this BBC production. Later, in this same series, *The Moving Finger, A Murder is Announced,* and *A Pocketful of Rye* were adapted, followed by a second series comprising *Nemesis, Sleeping Murder, At Bertram's Hotel,* and *Murder at the Vicarage. 4.50 from Paddington* was adapted as a Christmas 'special' in 1987 and *A Caribbean Mystery* at Christmas 1989.

The authors are grateful for biographical information provided by Agatha Christie Ltd.

INTRODUCTION

1990 was the centenary of Agatha Christie's birth and there were numerous commemorations, including tours by travel companies of the sites connected with her novels, the most expensive being, of course, a journey on the Orient Express. If readers wanted to visit St Mary Mead, the home of Miss Marple, the nearest they could hope for were villages in the Home Counties of the kind that Christie knew as a child, some of which have retained, at great expense and with some local opposition, their Edwardian rural atmosphere. As Christie herself said as late as 1975, Miss Marple's village 'is as real to me as it could be – and indeed there are several villages remarkably like it, even in these days'. Miss Marple, or someone very like her, can also still be found in some of these villages because she represents what seems to be an enduring type, the English spinster. Her name, with its almost Wildean comic potential as a part of speech – 'I have been doing a spot of Marpling' – was inspired by a visit to an old and very English house in Cheshire, Marple Hall, which was shortly to be pulled down. Christie went to buy furniture and amongst other relics from this monument of a previous age, she salvaged a name: '[it was] a very *good* sale with fine old Elizabethan and Jacobean furniture, and at it I bought 2 Jacobean oak chairs which I still have – wanting a name for my "old maid" character, I called her Jane Marple' (Morgan, 1984: 176).

Although Miss Marple has many literary antecedents, some of the details of her characterization derive from Christie's

personal experience, from her memories of her Ealing grandmother – 'Auntie Grannie' – and her grandmother's friends:

> old ladies whom I have met in so many villages where I have
> gone to stay as a girl. Miss Marple was not in any way a picture of
> my grandmother; she was far more fussy and spinsterish than my
> grandmother ever was. But one thing she did have in common
> with her – though a cheerful person, she always expected the
> worst of everyone and everything, and was, with almost
> frightening accuracy, usually proved right . . . . I endowed Miss
> Marple with something of Grannie's powers of prophecy. There
> was no unkindness in Miss Marple, she just did not trust people.
> Though she expected the worst, she often accepted people
> kindly in spite of what they were.
>
> (*Auto*: 449–50)

Christie had already written nine detective novels before the
first Miss Marple novel, *The Murder at the Vicarage*, was published
in 1930, and had created several detectives: Hercule Poirot,
Tommy and Tuppence Beresford, and Superintendent Battle.
Altogether, she was to write more than seventy detective stories
(and a handful of 'straight' novels), of which seventeen were
Miss Marple volumes. Miss Marple was to remain a favourite
detective with Christie, more so than Poirot who grew tedious
and whom she tried on several occasions to kill off. She resisted
the suggestion that Poirot and Marple should meet:

> *why* should they? I am sure they would not enjoy it at all. Hercule
> Poirot, the complete egoist, would not like being taught his
> business by an elderly spinster lady. He was a professional sleuth,
> he would not be at home at all in Miss Marple's world.
>
> (*Auto*: 449)

Part of Miss Marple's appeal to Christie, and to her readers, was
that unlike Poirot, who is an outsider and usually a visitor in the
world of the crime, Miss Marple belongs to the criminal society,
which in her case is pared down to the microcosm of a village.
It is of the essence of Miss Marple's amateur status that she is a
member of the community she will investigate, that, unlike
professional detectives, she doesn't have to be 'called in' from
an outside world. As Christie said of Miss Sheppard, Miss

Marple's predecessor in *The Murder of Roger Ackroyd*, 'I liked the part she played in village life: and I liked the idea of village life reflected through the life of the doctor and his masterful sister' (*Auto:* 449). Miss Marple's integration into the village community makes of her a greater moral force than if she came from outside to solve the crime; not only is the criminal one of us (for it is rare in Christie for the murderer to be a stranger) but the detective is one of us too, and her continued presence reminds us of the nearness and inevitability of retribution. If Poirot is a *deus ex machina* as a detective, Miss Marple is a kind of social conscience, dormant most of the time but always there, watchful and easily roused. That Christie regarded her detective stories in these moral terms is evident in her comments in her *Autobiography*:

> The detective story was the story of the chase; it was also very much a story with a moral; in fact it was the old Everyman Morality Tale, the hunting down of Evil and the triumph of Good. At that time, the time of the 1914 war, the doer of evil was not a hero: the *enemy* was wicked, the *hero* was good: it was as crude and as simple as that . . . I was, like everyone else who wrote books or read them, *against* the criminal and *for* the innocent victim.
>
> (*Auto:* 452)

She goes on to discuss the kinds of detective fiction that a writer can choose – the light-hearted thriller, the intricate story with an involved plot, for instance – and mentions a third kind which obviously stands high in her estimation. This is 'the detective story that has a kind of passion behind it – that passion being to help save innocence. Because it is *innocence* that matters, not *guilt*' (*Auto:* 453).

These comments were written when Christie was an old woman and have the benefit of hindsight and are, in any case, part of a tirade against wickedness and modern leniency towards it. Yet it is possible to see the Marple stories, more than the Poirot ones, as the Morality Tales Christie describes here, and also to see in them a development from early light-heartedness, as in *The Murder at the Vicarage*, through the involved plotting of *A Murder is Announced*, to a later, darker type of detective fiction which has 'a kind of passion behind it'. *Nemesis* and *Sleeping Murder*, both of which are concerned to exonerate those who have been wrongly accused, are examples of this 'passionate' side to Christie's work.

As we shall see, Jane Marple similarly develops throughout the novels from a rather comic, gossipy old lady into a much more formidable figure, a Nemesis who becomes an avenger of the innocent and Christie's instrument of justice in the detective novel of passion. What better figure to choose to defend the innocent than that admonitory figure of childhood, of fairy-stories and the morality tale: the maiden aunt, the spinster schoolteacher, the wise woman of the village? Relieved of sexuality and undistracted by close emotional bonds, such a figure cannot but see things clearly and act impartially as an agent of moral law.

The inter-war period was the heyday of the spinster and it was also, as Christie implies, a propitious time for detective fiction. To deal with violence in a controlled, hygienic and intellectualized way, to hunt down evil and expel the criminal from the community, to make uncomplicated moral judgements and assessments of character as part of a game – these were the vicarious powers and securities that detective fiction must have offered to a society which had experienced in the 1914–1918 war all too many real deaths and had known unprecedented levels of violence. It seemed, moreover, a particularly favourable time for women's detective fiction; emboldened by their war-time experiences, and enjoying new equalities with men, women domesticated the detective genre and made it into a vehicle for their own ratiocinative and moral capacities. Christie's distinctive contribution to this feminization of the genre was the milieu of apparent ordinariness, the small, unexceptional community which nevertheless harbours a killer. In this respect the Miss Marple stories, with their village settings, gossipy tea-parties and other old-maidish pursuits are the most characteristic fictions that Christie wrote.

The notion of an ordinary world disrupted by a killer, who is sometimes a person one knows, was foreshadowed for Christie in a recurrent nightmare she suffered as a child. It is tempting to see the need to exorcize 'The Gunman' nightmare, which she describes in *Unfinished Portrait* as well as in her *Autobiography*, as the origin of all her detective fiction. The nightmare itself has a psychological formula similar to a characteristic Christie novel, particularly a Marple one:

> I called him The Gunman because he carried a gun, not because I was frightened of his shooting me, or for any reason connected with the gun. The gun was part of his appearance, which seems to me now to have been that of a Frenchman in grey-blue uniform . . . and the gun was some old-fashioned kind of musket. It was his mere presence that was frightening. The dream would be quite ordinary – a tea-party, or a walk with various people, usually a mild festivity of some kind. Then suddenly a feeling of uneasiness would come. There was someone – someone *who ought not to be there* – a horrid feeling of fear: and then I would see him – sitting at the tea-table, walking along the beach, joining in the game. His pale blue eyes would meet mine, and I would wake up shrieking . . . . The Gunman was not always in costume. Sometimes, as we sat around a tea-table, I would look across at a friend, or a member of the family, and I would suddenly realise it was *not* Dorothy or Phyllis or Monty, or my mother or whoever it might be. The pale blue eyes in the familiar face met mine – under the familiar appearance. *It was really the Gunman.*
>
> (*Auto*: 36)

A 'mild festivity' is the occasion for many of Christie's murders and the *frisson* her novels give stems from a recognition that danger is not necessarily from without but is part of everyday life, the murderer is one of us. In detective fiction the nightmare is playfully evoked and then dispelled by the discovery and capture of the criminal. For the reader it can become an addictively reassuring process, as the huge sales of Christie's novels testify. It is also a highly conservative process because, generally speaking, the world that is reconstructed after the exposure of the criminal is one in which stable and idealized social relations, including traditional class and gender divisions, are upheld and property is restored to its rightful inheritors. As Cora Kaplan says, Christie, and the other Queens of Crime of the inter-war period, are purveyors of nostalgia, often defending in their fiction 'a social order that is decidedly on the wane if it has not actually disappeared from the real world some decades before' (Kaplan, 1986: 18–19).

If the detective story trades in nostalgia and assurance, it also has an appeal which is perhaps even more fundamental, and which has to do with the act of reading itself. This is a feature which the surprise bestseller of recent years, Umberto Eco's *The Name of the Rose*, has exploited. This novel is set in a library; the detective, Brother William, is aided by the unique possession of a pair of spectacles, and the murders revolve around a lost text by Aristotle. In other words, it is a (detective) novel about reading and writing and in its highly self-conscious way it suggests that reading is a process of detection. The detective story is, therefore, reading at its most basic, a paradigm of what is entailed when we open a book at the beginning and track it down to its conclusion. At least as far as the traditional novel is concerned, reading involves following a plot as a detective follows the narrative of the criminal's actions; signs must be read, clues picked up and remembered, characters assembled and judged on the basis of the evidence. In an 'ordinary' novel, these activities are disguised by the realism of the text but they are nevertheless there as readerly functions without which we could not make sense of the story, could not solve its mystery. In detective fiction this skeleton of the reading activity is its most prominent feature and the detective is a kind of surrogate author who conducts us (not always with entire reliability) through the narrative terrain.

Additionally, there takes place in the detective story an exaggerated if rudimentary Aristotelian (*pace The Name of the Rose*) catharsis in which the reader is purged by pity and terror and in which is also traced a narrative graph of crisis and resolution. Such a graph is common to comedy and tragedy alike, but in detective fiction it follows so obvious a contour as to afford a curious satisfaction. Like watching shadow puppets, or Punch and Judy, it is not texture, density or complexity which gives it appeal but the stark definition of emotion and action; here is the human story at its most basic and profoundly simple. The narrative contour of a detective story, for all its elaboration of clues and sub-plots, has a similarly satisfying archetypal simplicity.

Because the reading act is so much on the surface in detective fiction, this means that the reader's engagement with the text is direct and active. Detective novels – Christie's more than most – often are simply written, have short chapters and little scene-setting description, and their characterization is stereotypical. This is not necessarily to say that they are easy – they frequently demand an astute and concentrated attention to detail – but they do give pre-eminence to narrative, to constructing a sequence of events which explains the catastrophe, the murder. Almost equally with the detective, the reader is engaged in this construction of the narrative and can concentrate on it without having to bother very much about other fictional elements, such as complex psychology in the characters, or social realism, which muddy the reading of straight novels. As we point out in Chapter One, detective fiction endorses a highly individualistic ideology, not least because the reader, in attempting to solve the crime along with the detective, is engaged in a kind of do-it-yourself narrative, and is actively involved in the essential process of story-telling.

Perhaps this accounts for the addictive appeal of detective novels, and also their disposability. Any jumble sale will yield ranks of discarded detective stories (along with other formulaic narratives such as the Romance and the Western) from which eager addicts will snatch their favourite authors, and then recycle them at the next jumble sale. W.H. Auden comments on both the addictive and the ephemeral nature of the genre when he says that once he has begun a detective story, 'I cannot work or sleep till I have finished it [but] I forget the story as soon as I have finished it, and have no wish to read it again' (Auden, 1963: 146). What also may happen is that one cannot remember who the murderer is; the sequence of events and the criminal situation are clear enough but after a while the crucial figure of the murderer has faded from mind, the Gunman has retreated into the unconscious to await the next nightmare. Perhaps we forget the murderer, and indeed the whole story, because we do not want the story ever to be quite finished so that, Scheherazade-like, it will have to be told again, with variations of course, but basically the same narrative of pursuit and capture in which we are thrillingly but safely in charge.

In Miss Marple, all these readerly psychic needs of reassurance and autonomy find their apotheosis. As a spinster, that despised and marginalized figure of patriarchal society, she is a humble, amateur detective with whom identification, or even superiority, is readily achieved; surely, what she does, we could do also, we too could be a detective and bring order to a world temporarily thrown into chaos? Moreover, she represents the world of stability she protects and which, however delusively, we wish to preserve and have restored to us. She is Auntie–Grannie offering the comforts of cowslip wine, camomile tea, shops where you were served personally by a regular assistant, and firm but kindly government. She also seems to represent a nostalgic rural world of recognizable types and established hierarchies, where there is plenty of leisure, no real hardship, little work to do (unless one is a vicar, a doctor, or a servant), and the companionableness of a close-knit (if gossipy) community. It is interesting that Miss Marple's recent renaissance, particularly as far as television is concerned, has occurred during the Thatcher decade; are not the Victorian values she apparently upholds what we have been encouraged to espouse? And the individualism that is the core ideology of classical detective fiction, is this not the philosophy of the enterprise culture? It is also, perhaps, not too far-fetched to see in Miss Marple's certitudes and conservatism, something of Mrs Thatcher herself; a nation that has taken to one, has also taken to the other.

Chapter One

WOMEN WRITERS AND THE GOLDEN AGE OF DETECTIVE FICTION

IN 1928, Dorothy L. Sayers compiled a collection of short detective stories and concluded her introductory essay by celebrating the status and quality of detective fiction at that time: 'The average detective-novel to-day is extremely well written, and there are few good living writers who have not tried their hand at it at one time or another' (Sayers, in Winks, 1980: 83). Although this benign view of the genre was shared by other writers – Robert Graves and Alan Hodge, for instance – there were those who were appalled by its increasing popularity. Q.D. Leavis noted that 'an inordinate addiction to light reading' had been taken as a sign of vice in the nineteenth century but by the time she was writing *Fiction and the Reading Public* (1932) so degenerate had educated taste become that the keenest devotees of detective fiction were the educated classes – scientific men, clergymen, lawyers, businessmen – who 'in the last century would have been the guardians of the public conscience in the matter of mental self-indulgence' (Leavis, 1932: 50). Q.D. Leavis's sense of a world run mad on vicarious crime is upheld by the readership percentages of the lending libraries. At W.H. Smith's, a quarter of the novels available were crime novels, romances making up half the stock and adventure stories the last quarter. But a more lowbrow library would include up to 45 per cent detective stories among its titles (Beauman 1983: 173–4).

The period between the wars, when the crime story became a major popular genre, has come to be known as the Golden

Age of detective fiction. This description misleadingly suggests a homogeneous and 'classic' body of writing. In fact, the detective novel sprang from a range of different backgrounds and produced diverse detectives and differing ideologies of detection. Poe's Paris-based stories show an austere and remote detective (Auguste Dupin) whereas Conan Doyle's Sherlock Holmes is a flamboyant figure involved in sensational plots. In the inter-war period, the humorous detachment of the crime-puzzle novels of Sayers and Christie contrasts strongly with American hard-boiled realism and the cynical attitudes of a private eye like Marlowe or the avuncular compassion of Simenon's Maigret. The rural, middle-class society depicted in most Christie novels is totally different from the big-city squalor and scepticism of Dashiell Hammett. Throughout its history, it seems, the detective novel has found a successful place for itself within a variety of cultural contexts from upper-class Victorian London to Prohibition America. Lately, it has become a vehicle of modern feminism in the novels of Amanda Cross, Rebecca O'Rourke, Valerie Miner and others. The detective novel has conveyed all these very different cultures and interpretations of life and has obviously made such adaptations successfully.

It may seem surprising that such diverse types of writing should find a place within a literary genre which is as notoriously defined and institutionalized as the detective novel. For it is the case that both its authors and its critics have been obsessed by a prescriptive desire to regulate the detective novel's form and establish its definition. This belief in codification is understandable because certain features have persisted throughout the historical changes and in spite of the diversity of types within the genre. These constant factors, which may be called the literary core of the genre, concern the relationship between two individuals, the detective and the criminal, a relationship which involves a battle of wits: even in its most violent manifestations, detective fiction is never merely a shoot-out between detective and criminal but always involves a test of cunning and deduction. The conflict between the detective and the criminal also represents, however ambivalently, an opposition between right and wrong, order and disorder. These elements are so presented as to constitute, to varying degrees, a literary game in which the reader is invited, indeed required, to join.

This limited literary code, present in all detective stories, can be traced to the rise of a strong, moneyed bourgeoisie in the eighteenth and nineteenth centuries. Its ascent was accompanied by major changes in social relations. For the first time, the ownership of capital started to control the upwards and downwards mobility within society rather than class status based on the ownership of land. Detective stories clearly reflect this concern for capital, new in the eighteenth century and a dominant influence in the nineteenth; in particular, they are concerned with the effect of money on personal relations and the acquisition of possessions and their legitimate inheritance through the generations. The crimes in detective fiction are usually crimes against wealth and property; murder threatens to make the wrong person inherit, theft withdraws capital from its owner. These crimes are a corruption of normal financial transactions and consequently constitute a central anxiety in capitalist society which the detective story addresses.

This concern with property and capital is matched in importance in the ideology of the detective novel by the growth of individualism in capitalist society. As Stephen Knight (1980) has pointed out, an interest in crime and the apprehension of criminals can be traced back at least as far as *The Newgate Calendar* (c. 1774). When compared to the later detective genre, however, this early crime writing rests on different ideological assumptions. Painstaking detective work is significantly absent: when the crime has been committed, 'some men come up' and immediately identify and seize the culprit. This society is already interested in capitalist transactions but it is still a firmly organic and monolithic community, or at least these stories want us to believe so. Consequently, no sleuthing is necessary; the culprits betray themselves, they stand out because their crime has put them outside the Christian community. And the community as an entity reacts and punishes.

The growth of liberalism in the eighteenth century, however, shifted the emphasis of the reigning ideology on to a strain which had to an extent always been present in western society: the importance of the individual. Liberalism now foregrounded the individual, his or her situation or needs, and, as becomes obvious in a nineteenth-century writer like J.S. Mill, his or her rationality. Mill's 'On Liberty' (1859) champions the belief that the rational human being, who undertakes logical, reasoned actions, is now an attainable reality. Romanticism had also bolstered the ascendancy of the individual, even if it stressed a capacity for sensibility rather than, and often in reaction to, this formidable belief in rationality. But Romanticism also added hero-status to the individual who now stood magnified, in isolation, out of or in opposition to society. Drawing on ingredients from these twin nineteenth-century strands of Romanticism and rationalism, a new individual arose in literature: the detective.

It is generally agreed that Edgar Allan Poe's *The Murders in the Rue Morgue* (1841) was the first detective fiction in English. Poe would not have thought of himself as a detective writer; he was writing in a tradition of Gothic horror tales which included the crime story. Nevertheless he can lay claim to originating the detective story because, in the figure of Auguste Dupin, he introduced what has become the distinguishing feature of the genre, namely, the detective. Dupin, like his more famous successor, Sherlock Holmes, whose first appearance was in *A Study in Scarlet* (1887), represents the power of the controlling, investigative intelligence to restore order to a world temporarily thrown into chaos by the actions of the criminal. Dupin and Holmes are the masters of logic who are the self-appointed guardians of the money society, and who, within carefully defined limits, look after its moral welfare. These characteristics, and the romantic qualities of isolation and superiority which Dupin and Holmes exhibit, are developed, sometimes with ironic modifications, in Chandler's grim sleuths as well as in Hercule Poirot, Lord Peter Wimsey, and such present-day heroes as P.D. James's Adam Dalgliesh.

Romanticism, rationalism, and individualism within bourgeois society are, then, the conditions in which the detective genre came to birth and they provide its core ideology. The basic plot-formula resulting from this ideology involves a crime-mystery committed against property or inheritance which is solved by the hero-detective who is the guardian of capitalist society. This core ideology and its structuring narrative pattern, which are present in all, or most, detective stories, can be adapted to the needs of a particular period and a particular society. In the hard-boiled novels of Raymond Chandler or Dashiell Hammett, for instance, the rational investigation of a crime is strained by the need for a sensational, action-packed plot in tune with the mood of America during the Depression and Prohibition. The core ideology of the genre is thus augmented by a sub-ideology. During the era in which Agatha Christie came to fame the detective story in England developed its own variations and forged a sub-ideology so marked and popular as to earn it the designation of 'classical' or 'Golden Age'. And it was as writers of classical or Golden Age detective fiction that women were to prove so very successful.

What characterized the classical detective novel of the interbellum, and what its authors strove hard to institute, was the notion of the genre as a puzzle or a game operating honestly within rules. Some idea of this kind had been present to Conan Doyle in his conception of Holmes: thinking of previous detective stories

> it struck me what nonsense they were, to put it mildly, because for getting the solution of the mystery, the authors always depended on some coincidence. This struck me as not a fair way of playing the game, because the detective ought really to depend for his successes on his own mind and not on merely adventitious circumstances which do not, by any means, always occur in real life.
>
> (Quoted in Knight, 1980: 67)

But although Holmes is rational and empirical – 'You know my method. It is founded upon the observance of trifles', he says – his rationality is mysterious, superhuman almost, and the reader is left out of the detection process, trailing along, Watson-like, in the wake of Holmes's genius. In the classical detective novel of the inter-war period, the hitherto passive reader is invited to search along with the sleuth: democracy comes to the detective story. 'I think each one of us in his secret heart fancies himself as Sherlock Holmes', says the vicar in *The Murder at the Vicarage* and if this is true, at least for those reading the novel, then Christie and her Golden Age contemporaries provided the material to indulge this fancy.

This democratization was a major impulse in the foundation in 1932 of the Detection Club with G.K. Chesterton, E.C. Bentley and Dorothy L. Sayers among its founding members. The Club had a constitution and rules, and an election ceremony, allegedly composed by Sayers and Chesterton, in which members swore an oath promising that their detectives would 'well and truly detect the crimes presented to them' without reliance on 'Divine Revelation, Feminine Intuition . . . Mumbo Jumbo, Jiggery-Pokery, Coincidence or the Act of God'. Members of the Club also wrote essays – such as 'Twenty Rules for Writing Detective Stories' by S.S. Van Dine, 'A Defence of Detective Stories' by G.K. Chesterton, and Dorothy L. Sayers's introductions to *The Omnibus of Crime* and *Great Tales of Detection* – which aimed both to regularize and dignify the detective story and to emphasize the new aspects in its ideology, the idea of the game, the puzzle, and the notion of fair play. The Club was also concerned to stress the realism of the genre, its relevance to the ordinary lives of its readers.

Thus the classical detective story sets its crime, usually a murder relating to money and property, in the milieu of respectable, bourgeois life. The detection of the crime is intellectualized into a game involving the reading of signs, a game which is played by several sets of players in a kind of semiotic hierarchy. At the lowest level of cognizance are the characters in the novel, most of whom, including the murderer, are deliberately or unwittingly laying clues of their own in relation to other characters, which each partially or totally misreads. Next in the chain are the novel's readers who are reading the clues so that they can solve the mystery themselves. Then there is the expert games-player, the detective, who is reading the signs in a superior but not a superhuman way. Finally, of course, there is the author, the supreme puzzle-maker in the hierarchy; like a chess grand-master playing several boards at once, the author determines the progress of each game that is being played, and in one of the games, the one with the reader, there is, according to the rules laid down in classical detective fiction, a special relationship of what might be called honest deception. The reader can be fooled and led up the garden path (indeed, part of the charm of reading detective fiction lies in just such hazards) but this must be fairly done: coincidence must not be excessive; intuition should be minimal; facts, such as those concerning poisons, the geography of a place, or the time it takes to do things, should be accurate. Above all, clues should not be arbitrary: they can be right or wrong, but they should not be merely random, meaningless, autonomous. In opposition to real life, the detective's world is semiotically fully determined; every clue is significant, pointing towards the eventual discovery of the criminal and also towards the exculpation of the innocent. This gives the pleasant illusion that reality is intelligible and can therefore be controlled. If the author is incompetent or unfair, this constitutes a 'crime' against the reader; it destroys the subtle power hierarchy upon which detective fiction depends and removes the comforting sense of the ability of logic to make sense of reality. In really satisfying detective fiction of the classic type, the author must win the game with the reader whilst at the same time demonstrating that the truth of the crime is entirely accessible to anyone with logical powers only a little above the ordinary. The burden of this double manoeuvre usually requires an apparently impossible denouement to the story in which surprise and logical inevitability are equally present.

To Dorothy L. Sayers, who was one of the most theoretical of the interbellum detective writers, this emphasis on the puzzle and on fair play was a revolutionary development. In earlier detective fiction, like some of the Sherlock Holmes stories, clues were introduced to revive a flagging plot and there was a reliance on coincidence and intuition to an improbable degree. This kind of authorial arbitrariness was no longer allowable; the genre was controlled and formulaic, governed by rules such as Ronald Knox's 'A Detective Story Decalogue' which included the instructions that 'No accident must ever help the detective, nor must he ever have an unaccountable intuition which proves to be right', and 'The detective must not light on any clues which are not instantly produced for the inspection of the reader', as well as more precise regulations such as 'Not more than one secret passage is allowable' and 'The stupid friend of the detective, the Watson, must not conceal any thoughts which pass through his mind; his intelligence must be slightly, but very slightly, below that of the average reader' (Knox, in Winks, 1980: 200–2). Knox is exaggerating the formula in order to mock it but he nevertheless points to a serious intention of these interbellum writers to dignify the detective genre by promoting its rational qualities.

The rationality and logic which are of prime importance to the detective novel of this period actually involve a double display of logic. The rationality of the detective repeats the thinking of the criminal; the criminal's plot to commit the crime and evade discovery are shadowed by the detective's tracing of this plot and its exposure in the final act. There are thus two complementary and dialectical aspects of the plot developing simultaneously, in which the reader's attention moves forward to the resolution of the crime and backwards towards its origins. In this way, total control is established over the crime at the heart of the action. At the end of a classical detective novel, both the crime's past and the criminal's future are completely known and defined. The reader thus participates in an illusion of domination over past and future. This insistence on logic is an assertion of power, an ideological affirmation that the rational individual can regulate events. However lighthearted, this wish for control over the surrounding reality underlies both the reading and writing of detective fiction.

Yet control only exists in the face of disorder. Much of the pleasure of reading classical detective fiction lies in the possibility of the control over reality slipping, and logic not being able to make sense of a mass of information, only some of which will lead to the truth of the crime.

'It's very interesting', [Miss Marple] said with a sigh, 'all the different things that people say – and think. The things they see – or think that they see. And all so complex, nearly all so trivial and if one thing isn't trivial, it's so hard to spot which one – like a needle in a haystack.'

(*MIA*: ch. 8)

The task of the detective, shadowed by the reader, is to take account of everything everybody says and from it to discover truth, the needle in the haystack. Before this happens, red herrings are introduced and truth is temporarily shown as complicated, relative and not to be readily ascertained. The detective story thus plays with the idea of the breakdown of meaning, only to conclude triumphantly that it does exist; there is a needle in a haystack. Dorothy L. Sayers's seventh novel, *Five Red Herrings*, explicitly makes the point by providing all six of her suspects with plausible scenarios for the murder of a fellow painter. Five of these are misreadings but until that is discovered, there is the fear of *all* versions being equally true – or untrue. This fissure at the heart of logic, the fact that logic can lead to many 'truths' in a world of multiple meanings, is quickly covered up by the success of the sleuth but not before the writer and reader of detective fiction have enjoyed a *frisson* at the possibility that logic may not be able to make sense of the complexities of existence.

In its emphasis upon the detection of crime as a game of logic, classical detective fiction creates a paradox in which violent emotion and action – the crime – is treated in a remote, intellectualized, and even humorous way. Comparing the genre to a dissecting-table, Sayers insisted on a 'dispassionate eye' on the part of the author, a 'detached attitude' so that the analysis of facts and the piecing together of clues would be unaffected by authorial sentiment (Sayers, in Winks, 1980: 77). The result is what George Grella calls a 'thriller of manners . . . . A formal minuet leading to an inescapable conclusion, as mannered and unreal as the masque, the sonnet, or the drawing room farce' (Grella, in Winks, 1980: 101). Indeed, the detective novel often resembles the comedy of manners in its preference for conventional characters and situations, its intricate, intellectualized plot, and its epigrammatic dialogue. Many of Christie's characters and their utterances would not be out of place in an Oscar Wilde play: 'Selina Blake is the nicest woman imaginable. Her herbaceous borders are simply marvellous. . . . And she's frightfully generous with cuttings', says Mrs Bantry in *The Body in the Library*, and this mockingly tells us about both Mrs Bantry and the world she inhabits, a comfortable world in which moral character is equated with gardening, and which is now under threat from the crime. A murder such as occurs in this novel, where a rather tarty young woman is found dead in respectable Colonel Bantry's library, creates a thrill typical of Christie's novels where so often social embarrassment surrounds the scene of the crime. As testified by the detective novel that Mrs Bantry has been reading, *The Clue of the Broken Match*, the body-in-the-library is a convention – 'Bodies are always being found in libraries in books. I've never known a case in real life', says Colonel Bantry – which Christie is not afraid to exploit for its social and comic implications. 'The library in question must be a highly orthodox and conventional library. The body . . . must be a wildly improbable and highly sensational body', she wrote in her foreword to the novel. In this collision of the conventional with the sensational arises a class and sexual unease whereby Colonel Bantry is suspected, if not of the murder, then of a liaison with the victim. Although this is humorous it is also a danger to the settled order of St Mary Mead in which the Bantrys occupy an honoured position. So many of the murders in Christie's novels occur amidst just such a socially embarrassing situation: an awkward sherry party in *A Murder is Announced*, a conflict-torn reception in *The Mirror Crack'd from Side to Side*, and the possible misappropriation of the church funds in *The Murder at the Vicarage*. The crime thus comes to seem merely one further aspect of social inconvenience, an additional example of bad taste and not the emotional and pitiful occurrence it would be in reality. Even the description of the dead body of the victim is perfunctory, stylized and brisk, as in *The Murder at the Vicarage* where Colonel Protheroe is discovered:

sprawled across my writing table in a horrible unnatural position. There was a pool of some dark fluid on the desk by his head, and it was slowly dripping on to the floor with a horrible drip, drip, drip . . . . The man was dead – shot through the head.

(*MV*: ch. 5)

Even less time is spent on Mr Fortescue in *A Pocketful of Rye*: 'behind his desk [he] seemed contorted with agony. His convulsive movements were alarming to watch . . . . Even as she came up to him, his body was convulsed in a painful spasmodic movement.' In both novels, the discovery of the corpse is over within eight lines and the detection elements of the plot – the arrival of the doctor and the police and the gathering of suspects and evidence – have overtaken the act of violence. As Stephen Knight says:

> the artificiality of the puzzle-creation, so willingly accepted by readers, in itself euphemises events. The game-like features of the novel are forceful enough to dilute the real strength of the threats that are played with. Only the most technically and aesthetically strained processes can present so complete a puzzle, and this in itself suggests that ordinary life will not be so testing and allows the reader's fears of others – and even of the self – to exercise and dissolve themselves in a controlled, hygienic environment.
>
> (Knight, 1980: 127)

This neutralizing of the murder into an intellectual and comic act is aided by the fact that the victim is usually not an attractive person or one for whom the reader has much sympathy or knows anything about. Colonel Protheroe in *The Murder at the Vicarage*, for example, is a domestic tyrant and a pompous and overbearing member of the village community and almost everyone, including the vicar, thinks how much they would like him out of the way; naturally he is the murder victim and there are numerous suspects who are guilty in thought if not in deed. Mr Fortescue in *A Pocketful of Rye* is similarly unattractive, of a type Christie seems particularly to have disliked: 'a large flabby man with a gleaming bald head' who was rude and domineering in manner and 'a definite bully'. The exceptions to this rule of the unsympathetic victim, as far as Christie's Marple stories are concerned, are *Sleeping Murder* and *Nemesis* where the victim in each case is a young woman whose desire to escape from the possessive love of a relative leads to her murder. Both these murders have been committed long ago in the past and there is a sense of regret and melancholy to these two novels which marks them out from Christie's earlier and more comic crime stories.

If the emotional impact of murder is usually strictly controlled within intellectual and comic limits, this is also true of other factors which are potentially disturbing, particularly those concerning class relations. For although the detective story deals in unease, it does so in reassuring ways, and most classical detective fiction is careful to avoid any suggestion of class conflict. The servants in Christie's novels are usually stupid and amiable, and the utmost rebellion they show is in 'flouncing', as Mary does in *The Murder at the Vicarage*, or in leaving Miss Marple's tutelage to work in a cafe or to try to find a boyfriend, as the credulous Gladys does in *A Pocketful of Rye*. Particular care in this respect is taken in regard to the criminal who is rarely of the working class. Although a tramp or a butler is sometimes suspected in Christie's novels, eventually the murderer is found to be middle class, 'one of us', a property-owning individual or at least one who believes themselves to be entitled to own property. S.S. Van Dine stresses this when he writes in 'Twenty Rules for Writing Detective Stories' that the culprit must not be a servant, who in real life would readily come under suspicion, but 'a worthwhile person' who would not 'ordinarily' be suspect (Van Dine, in Haycroft, 1976: 189–94). This exclusion of servant-murderers subdues any middle-class anxieties concerning the working class; a servant or working-class culprit would make the detective story too political, too subversive of the class domination which was part and parcel of its ideology.

Of course, to have the criminal 'one of us' can be equally or more disturbing. Most detective novels derive some of their tension from the idea that murder or betrayal can be committed by people one trusts, even a wife or husband, children or close friends. In recalling her first thoughts of writing a detective novel, and her decision that it must be 'an *intime* murder . . . it would have to be all in the family, so to speak . . . . A husband could murder his wife – that seemed to be the most usual kind of murder' (*Auto*: 261), Christie was tapping an anxiety every human being feels at some level towards lovers, friends, or relatives, or rather, towards their individuality. It is the Gunman nightmare: we can never entirely identify with the Other; absolute trust, a perfect mutual understanding is impossible. Instead, we are forced to live within a sociable compromise of uncertainty. A modern detective novelist, Ruth Rendell, has written of this precarious compromise in *The Veiled One* where the title refers to the sudden awareness that a person's closest relative may change beyond recognition, a mother become unrecognizable to her son. The motif of mistaken or falsified identity occurs in many Christie novels but the anxieties it arouses are allayed in the final disclosures concerning the crime. In *A Murder is Announced* a nephew and a niece turn out to be impostors, and in *A Pocketful of Rye* the in-laws are really children of acquaintances seeking revenge. The reassurance comes into play once these shocks of recognition have been weathered. When everybody's identity has been established without a shadow of doubt, it becomes easy to identify the motive for murder and hence the killer. After this, a more secure world than ever before is created because the truth about everyone has been ascertained and any unease and doubt has been located and expelled in the figure of the murderer. Thus a very real fear of 'the veiled one' is transposed in classical detective fiction into a game where the discovery of identity leads logically to the ridding of society of its destructive and disturbing elements.

Such psychological factors lie at the heart of W.H. Auden's explanation for the curious popularity of detective fiction. He suggests that the detective story is a reformulation of 'the dialectic of innocence and guilt'. The typical reader, in his opinion, is someone who 'suffers from a sense of sin' to whom the detective story appeals because it is about 'innocence which is discovered to contain guilt; then a suspicion of being the guilty one; and finally a real innocence from which the guilty other has been expelled' (Auden, 1963: 146). Christie often plays with this notion of the untrustworthiness of everyone, even of oneself; it is particularly notable, notorious even, in *The Murder of Roger Ackroyd* where the most trusted character, in a sense, is revealed as the murderer. Poirot drives the point home when he says:

> 'Let us take a man – a very ordinary man. A man with no idea of murder in his heart. There is in him somewhere a strain of weakness – deep down. It has so far never been called into play. Perhaps it never will be – and if so he will go to his grave honoured and respected by everyone. But let us suppose that something occurs. He is in difficulties . . . '.
>
> (*MRA*: ch. 17)

Implicit in these statements is the idea of the detective story as a moral fable of some kind. 'In detective stories virtue is always triumphant. They're the purest literature we have', says Dorothy L. Sayers' Lord Peter Wimsey, and this folklorist view of detective fiction is shared by several of the Golden Age writers:

> By dealing with the unsleeping sentinels who guard the outposts of society, it tends to remind us that we live in an armed camp, making war with a chaotic world, and that the criminals, the children of chaos, are nothing but traitors within our gates.
>
> (Chesterton, in Haycraft, 1976: 5)

This sense of the simplicity of evil, and the reliability with which it can be defeated, makes for a superficial and reassuring morality which is in contradiction to the apparent realism of classical detective fiction. For Chesterton also believed that detective fiction 'is the earliest and only form of popular literature in which is expressed some sense of the poetry of modern life': 'there is no stone in the street and no brick in the wall that is not actually a deliberate symbol, a message from some man'. Like Sayers, he seems to want the best of all worlds: the abstract puzzle, the morality tale, and the open-endedness and probability of realism. In fact, a skilful writer like Christie can straddle the contradiction with a patina of authenticity and topicality under cover of which both the puzzle-game and the moral fable can be worked out. How this is done can be seen in an extract from Christie's first successful novel, *The Murder of Roger Ackroyd*:

> Our village, King's Abbot, is, I imagine, very much like any other village. Our big town is Cranchester, nine miles away. We have a large railway station, a small post office, and two rival 'General Stores'. Able-bodied men are apt to leave the place early in life, but we are rich in unmarried ladies and retired military officers. Our hobbies and recreations can be summed up in the one word, 'gossip'.
>
> There are only two houses of any importance in King's Abbot. One is King's Paddock, left to Mrs Ferrars by her late husband. The other, Fernly Park, is owned by Roger Ackroyd. Ackroyd has always interested me by being a man more impossibly like a country squire than any country squire could really be. . . . Of course, Ackroyd is not really a country squire. He is an immensely successful manufacturer of (I think) wagon wheels. He is a man of nearly fifty, rubicond of face and genial of manner. He is hand in glove with the vicar, subscribes liberally to parish funds (though rumour has it that he is extremely mean in personal expenditure), encourages cricket matches, Lads' Clubs, and Disabled Soldiers' Institutes. He is, in fact, the life and soul of our peaceful village of King's Abbot.
>
> (*MRA*: ch. 2)

Slightly reminiscent of Thomas Hardy's Melstock or of Elizabeth Gaskell's Cranford, this description of the village borrows enough substance from its literary predecessors to make the reader accept it as a representation of a familiar, and therefore 'real', scene. As George Grella says, detective fiction presents us with a 'knowable universe' (Grella, in Winks, 1980: 101) and it is probably all the better if the knowledge it offers is from literature rather than life. The scene is set by a kind of shorthand; in this extract the village is given with stereotypical economy of detail of a traditional kind yet at the same time updated by sufficient topical information – Lads' Clubs and Disabled Soldiers' Institutes – to give a surface impression of being situated in modern life. The property and class relations are quickly established and ironic signals sent out regarding the plot which is to follow: Roger Ackroyd will soon no longer be the life (though he may be the soul) of the village and King's Abbot itself will no more be peaceful. Of course, it is self-consciously artificial; like Roger Ackroyd, it is more real than the real thing and with amazing sophistication Christie admits as much, and also admits that it doesn't really matter. As in a game of chess, where it is how the pieces move and not what they 'really' stand for that is important, so in Christie's novel the locations and characters bear only a shadowy relation to social conditions and historical events. Death, the war, poverty – the novel was published in 1926, the year of the General Strike – are evoked but rendered passive and safe in the detective game the novel enacts. As John G. Cawelti says, 'Character and atmosphere are reduced to the barest minimum and function only as necessary embodiments to the structure of detection and mystification' (Cawelti, in Winks, 1980: 193).

Similarly, although the plot in this novel unfolds around a mass of detail and tangible evidence, such as the inventory of objects in the drawer of Ackroyd's bureau, the plans of Ackroyd's house, and the room in which he died, all such material is tightly controlled and functional, giving the semblance of a recognizable social world but existing primarily to promote the various lines of enquiry of the crime-puzzle. Under this cover of 'realism', there is the assurance that the crime will be detected and that, as a result, good will prevail and the wrong-doer be brought to justice. Poirot provides the connecting assurance because, as George Grella says, 'this penchant for the tangible implies a world that can be interpreted by human reason, embodied in the superior intellect of the detective' (Grella, in Winks, 1980: 101). Through Poirot the clues are pieced together, the murderer discovered and expelled, and King's Abbot purged of its disruptive element: 'It was rather like a jig-saw puzzle to which everyone contributed their own little piece of knowledge or discovery. But their task ended there. To Poirot alone belongs the renown of fitting those pieces into their correct place' (*MRA*: ch. 14). The final piece to be fitted into the puzzle is the shocking disclosure that the murderer of Roger Ackroyd is not only respectable and respected but also truly unexpected. Although this was the novel that made

Christie's name, it alienated many of her readers; is it really playing the game to have the murderer and the detective so intertwined as to fool the reader as completely as *Roger Ackroyd*'s first readers were fooled? Christie's own prescription for a '*good* detective story' – 'that it must be somebody obvious but at the same time, for some reason, you would then find that it was *not* obvious, that he could not possibly have done it. Though really, of course, he *had* done it' (*Auto*: 262) – was almost too brilliantly carried out for the readers' comfort.

As *The Murder of Roger Ackroyd* demonstrates, Christie is typical of detective fiction writers in showing herself highly self-conscious of the genre she is writing in, sometimes disingen-uously so in making it appear a rather matter-of-fact and mechanical exercise. It is like cooking, she suggests in her author's foreword to *The Body in the Library*: 'a tennis pro, a young dancer, an artist, a girl guide, a dance hostess, etc. and serve up *à la* Miss Marple'. Or it is like a magician's sleight of hand, what Miss Marple calls 'misdirection' where the murderer, and the author, obscure or direct attention away from what is basically quite straightforward: 'Murders so often are quite simple – with an obvious rather sordid motive', Miss Marple says in *4.50 from Paddington*, where, after many red herrings, it is what Christie herself called 'the most usual kind of murder', a husband murders his wife. Christie frequently incorporates references in her novels to the conventions of detective fiction and this establishes an 'in-joke' relationship with the reader and also allows her ironically to play off her plot against the convention. In *The Body in the Library* Miss Marple is taken for a writer of detective stories by a small boy who is an avid reader of them: 'The most unlikely people, he knew, wrote detective stories. And Miss Marple, in her old-fashioned spinster's clothes, looked a singularly unlikely person.' Of course, he misses the even more unexpected point that she is the *detective*. Earlier in the same novel, the boy says to the police, 'Do you like detective stories? I do. I read them all, and I've got autographs from Dorothy L. Sayers and Agatha Christie and Dickson Carr and H.C. Bailey.' The field of reference for this sort of coterie joke can be quite wide; in *A Murder is Announced*, for instance, Miss Marple tentatively suggests the notion of 'the fall guy' which she has taken from 'one of Mr. Dashiell Hammett's stories. (I understand from my nephew Raymond that he is considered at the top of the tree in what is called the "tough" style of literature.)'. This novel, one of the best of the Marple stories, begins with an indication of how popular detective games were at the time by making use of a murder-game party which is announced in the newspaper:

> A murder is announced and will take place on Friday, October 29th . . . , at Little Paddocks at 6.30 p.m. Friends please accept this, the only intimation.

The announcement suggests both a wedding invitation and a funeral notice but all those who read it recognize it as a 'Murder Game', which is explained for the benefit of the uninitiated: 'You draw lots. One person's the murderer, nobody knows who. Lights out. Murderer chooses victim. The victim has to count twenty before he screams. Then the person chosen to be the detective takes charge. Questions everybody.' To base the initial murder scene on a popular social game of the time, itself based on the classical detective novel, is bringing the self-referencing full circle.

The popularity of the genre is clearly attested in references like these. They also serve as an assurance that it is all right to read such literature; schoolboys, respectable gardening ladies like Mrs Bantry, police inspectors and, most of all, vicars are found reading novels with titles like *A Stain on the Stairs* (*MV*) and *Death Does the Hat Trick* (*AMIA*). Although Q.D. Leavis could complain about the general lowering of reading standards, according to the novels themselves, such reading habits are at worst only a pardonable weakness and at best they affirm a solidarity between the reader and a character in the novel who is a respectable class model – a vicar or a retired colonel – and who is also reading detective fiction. Perhaps such identification was necessary because a whole class of relatively new readers, the working classes, were taking to the crime thriller, as distinct from the detective story, with alacrity. Leavis quotes a public librarian of the inter-war period as saying that if he put 200 more copies of Edgar Wallace's crime stories on the shelves, they would all be gone the same day (Leavis, 1932: 50). Christie and the other Crime Club writers were concerned to stake out a different territory from Wallace, to mark out a middle-class enclave within detective fiction in which the settings are refined and moneyed, and the plot relies on logic and wit rather than sensation and violence. It was an enclave in which women writers were to thrive, in fact, to make peculiarly their own.

There are four women detective writers of this period, sometimes called the Queens of Crime or the Quartet of Muses, who are still remembered and read today and who were highly instrumental in establishing the genre in its classic status: Agatha Christie, Dorothy L. Sayers, Ngaio Marsh and Margery Allingham. One might ask why these intelligent women of obvious literary gifts should turn to detective stories rather than other kinds of fiction.

In *A Very Great Profession* Nicola Beauman, who, incidentally, does not feature detective writers, says:

> The years between the wars were the heyday of fiction written by women. Novel writing was, finally, a respectable occupation . . . . Middle-class women had time, warmth, freedom from drudgery and an intelligence unsullied by the relentless and wearying monotony of housework.
>
> (Beauman, 1983: 6)

She could well have added that women also had increasing expertise. The war had opened up work opportunities and the knowledge that accompanied them; Christie is a case in point in her employment in a dispensary. There was also greater access to higher education so that women like Stella Benson or Naomi Mitchison, both of whom read history at university in the early 1920s, were better trained than their predecessors had been to write accurately researched historical novels. Yet in spite of increased opportunities and widening horizons, the majority of these writing women remained, as Beauman suggests, very much like their Victorian counterparts in being ladies, who wrote about the lives of ladies like themselves, often within a context of romance and domesticity. It is against this background of middle-class domestic fiction by women that the rise to prominence of the female detective writer must be placed. As Jessica Mann has pointed out, for the many women who took to writing detective fiction, and the much greater numbers who read it, it had assumed a new respectability, particularly by comparison with earlier and more sensational novelists such as Baroness Orczy (Mann, 1981: 32–8). Yet although they adhered to the same social milieu as contemporary romance writers, as detective novelists they could escape from or subordinate romance in the exercise of ratiocinative and game-playing faculties. Christie more than any of them shed the romantic element in her detective stories very quickly – 'I myself always found the love interest a terrible bore in detective stories . . . . To force a love motif into what should be a scientific process went much against the grain' (*Auto*: 266) – but even Sayers, who threads the love story of Harriet Vane and Peter Wimsey through several of her detective fictions, does not allow the romance to predominate, except in *Busman's Honeymoon*, the least skilful and the last (1937), which Sayers described as 'a love story with detective interruptions'. What the interbellum form of the genre offered to women writers, and their women readers, was the opportunity to remain within the respectable and domestic, to keep within the women's sphere, yet at the same time to use that sphere in a different way to satisfy different needs.

Christie herself was typical of the kind of woman who wrote and read detective fiction. Comfortable and protected as a child, educated informally and marrying young, she would probably not have taken paid employment if it had not been for the war when, after some VAD experience, she became an assistant in a dispensary and began to study for the examinations for the Apothecaries' Hall. As Janet Morgan explains, the work suited Christie's talents for codification and orderly thinking and her notebooks contain alphabetical lists of the 'appearance and properties of various substances, the sources from which they may be derived and the substances with which they are incompatible' (Morgan, 1984: 70). It was also here that she learned about poisons. In her *Autobiography* she recalls an incident which reveals her awareness of the different kinds of power people possess. Her superior, a man so incapable of being told he was wrong that she once destroyed some drugs rather than tell him he had wrongly prescribed them, one day showed her a piece of dark-coloured substance he carried in his pocket:

> 'It's curare', he said .... 'Interesting stuff .... Taken by the mouth it does you no harm at all. Enter the bloodstream, it paralyses and kills you .... Do you know why I carry it in my pocket?' 'No,' I said, 'I haven't the slightest idea ....' 'Well, you know', he said thoughtfully, 'it makes me feel powerful.' I looked at him then. He was a rather funny-looking little man, very roundabout and robin redbreast looking, with a nice pink face. There was a general air of childish satisfaction about him.
> (*Auto*: 260–1)

Christie used this incident in a novel of fifty years later, *The Pale Horse*; it is an illuminating insight into the respective power games each of these slightly marginalized people play: the insignificant man carrying a piece of death in his pocket, the woman writing about death.

But even literary murder and theft might seem unsuitable for the nicely brought up young women whom Christie represented. How could they know about the squalor and violence that usually accompany murder? Of course, they may well have known because several of them, including Christie, had had war experience and no murder could surpass in horror some of the war injuries they may have seen. But the assumption was that they didn't and shouldn't know, and their novels maintain the assumption. The bloodless and stylized quality of the English detective novel made crime acceptable to women writers and readers, and the conventions, the humour, and the ritualized settings neutralized gruesome and potentially offensive subject matter into elegant games befitting respectable women. By the time Christie began to write, the genre had also moved away considerably from the romantic admiration for activity so characteristic of the Sherlock Holmes stories towards a less heroic, more ordinary detective. By the interbellum, both the hero and the plot had become more moderate and domestic, so that women readers and writers were able to feel at ease with the relative homeliness of the crime story. With the advent of the four Queens of Crime the establishment of the sub-genre of what we might call feminized detective fiction is complete.

Primarily this depended on the kind of detective created by these authors. It is not merely that they make use of women sleuths and assistant sleuths – Harriet Vane, Miss Climpson, Troy Alleyn, Allingham's Amanda Fitton, Christie's Ariadne Olivier and, of course, Miss Marple – but also that their male detectives have a feminine appeal. Christie's Hercule Poirot, Dorothy L. Sayers's Peter Wimsey and Margery Allingham's Albert Campion are effeminate and frequently comic, a far cry from Sherlock Holmes or their contemporary, Marlowe, in the hard-boiled school, and this makes them approachable and endearing. Christie envisaged Poirot as 'a tidy little man. I could see him as a tidy little man, always arranging things, liking things in pairs, liking things square instead of round', and in *The Murder of Roger Ackroyd* he is introduced as having 'an egg-shaped head, partially covered with suspiciously black hair, two immense moustaches, and a pair of watchful eyes' and is absurdly throwing vegetable marrows over the garden wall. Poirot is little, vain, pompous and a foreigner, in particular a Belgian which, to the English mind, means being exceptionally insignificant, even for a foreigner. Margery Allingham's Campion is equally disarming; in *Police at the Funeral* he is described as 'a lank immaculate form surmounted by a pale face half obliterated by enormous horn-rimmed spectacles [and] an habitual expression of contented idiocy'. Similarly Sayers' Peter Wimsey, in *Whose Body?*, has a 'long amiable face [which] looked as if it had generated spontaneously from his top hat, as white maggots breed from Gorgonzola'. Even Ngaio Marsh's Inspector Roderick Alleyn, the only policeman amongst them, is languid and self-effacing and, like Wimsey and Campion, an aristocrat. Their noble birth appeals to the readers' snobbery; at the same time, and in this respect they are like Poirot, it casts them in the role of outsider in the usually middle-class world of the crime. The mixture of the effete, the exotic, and the comic that these outsiders present is a powerful disguise; they may look silly, they may appear vain and affected, but this is a surface which conceals their powers of reasoning and their quite ruthless quest for justice. It is easy to understand how such figures would appeal to women writers and readers; are not Poirot and his ilk very like women themselves – apparently trivial, but actually the ones who put the pattern together, who restore order to a shaken world?

How they do this is not through the lonely and almost superhuman activity of Sherlock Holmes, nor the dangerous violence of Marlowe. Albert Campion is polite and modest, happy to spend his time in apparently foolish ways. For all his reliance on 'the little grey cells of the mind', Poirot also is not a remote cerebralizer but a man who potters about amongst the evidence and chats to people in a fussy and friendly manner. Such detectives suggest to their readers that the identification of crime is within the power of ordinary people, and reading detective fiction of this kind becomes, in its light-hearted way, an empowering experience; although a Poirot, a Campion or a Marple may show the way, the impression is that crime detection is basically a do-it-yourself operation.

This becomes particularly the case for female readers when one of the sleuth's female assistants performs a piece of evidence collecting which only a woman can do: Harriet Vane in an Oxford women's college, for instance, or Miss Climpson trying to gain access to a dying woman by drinking her way through innumerable cups of coffee and tea in various teashops in order to befriend the woman's nurse. As we shall see in Chapter Three, it is Jane Marple who will make a speciality of such feminine activity and in so doing will become not the sleuth's assistant but the sleuth herself.

The situations in which these detectives operate is similarly accessible; often, the murder takes place in a family just a little higher up the social scale than the average middle-class reader so that whilst the social patterns are recognizable – what time tea is served, how well-brought-up girls dress, who can reasonably call on whom – there is the glamour that a little more money and a little more grandeur can bring and the greater temptation to crime they offer. Christie, in particular, is a shrewd judge of the gradations of wealth and social class and often uses Miss Marple, who is poor but well-bred, as a measure of both. Christie is also adept in the use of apparently ordinary and familiar backgrounds for her murder mysteries. Allingham and Marsh often venture into the glamourous worlds of fine art and the theatre and Sayers is at her best in the evocation of an unusual setting, such as the Oxford women's college in *Gaudy Night* or the bleak fen country of *The Nine Tailors*. But Christie locates her crime in what seems like a safe and known (in literature if not in life) society, what Colin Watson calls 'the little world of Mayhem Parva':

> a cross between a village and a commuters' dormitory in the South of England, self-contained and largely self-sufficient. It would have a well-attended church, an inn with reasonable accommodation for itinerant detective-inspectors, a village institute, library and shops – including a chemist's where weed killer and hair dye might conveniently be bought. The district would be rural, but not uncompromisingly so – there would be a good bus service for the keeping of suspicious appointments in the nearby town, for instance – but its general character would be sufficiently picturesque to chime with the English suburban dweller's sadly uninformed hankering after retirement to 'the country'.
>
> (Watson, 1971: 169–70)

Mayhem Parva, like King's Abbot, is peopled with stereotypes: the army, the church, and the medical profession are represented along with various widows and spinster ladies, a sprinkling of maids, butlers, and gardeners, and a few outsiders – parvenu wealthy ex-businessmen, an artist or writer, and sometimes a mysterious person who comes to live in Mayhem Parva, whose arrival is a source of curiosity to everyone and who is naturally pivotal to the crime and its detection. It is typically a female world of gossip and small intrigue – Cranford spiced with a murder puzzle – and thus reassuringly conservative for its female readership. Having invented this world in her very early novels, particularly in *The Murder of Roger Ackroyd*, Christie gave it a presiding genius, the quintessential Mayhem Parva figure of the well-bred, elderly English spinster, Miss Marple.

Yet if Miss Marple and St Mary Mead are nostalgic clichés, they are often given an astringent quality by a play of irony which points away from a too easy acceptance of the clichés, particularly clichés concerning women. Christie does this more than her contemporaries whose excursions into female independence invariably end in conventional submission to a male sleuth who also is, or becomes, the husband: Harriet Vane and Peter Wimsey, Agatha Troy and Roderick Alleyn. But Miss Marple, whilst never voicing feminist statements, is not only a genuinely independent woman but also the chief sleuth whom police inspectors hold in awe. In lesser ways, too, Christie upsets the stereotypes she makes use of; in *The Murder at the Vicarage*, for example, Inspector Slack says that the murderer must be a man because 'women never like fiddling about with firearms. Arsenic's more their line', yet a woman has shot Colonel Protheroe and has done it in cold blood as part of a rationally thought-out strategy. In *The Moving Finger*, after much suspicion has fallen on spinster women in the village, it emerges that the venomous letters have in fact been written by a man who wishes to marry the vacuously beautiful governess; men can commit 'women's crimes' whilst at the same time they are, stereotypically, fools over pretty women. (In this respect, Christie's novel is less conventional than Dorothy L. Sayers's *Gaudy Night* where the poison-letter writer turns out to be, after all, an embittered, spiteful woman.) In *They Do it with Mirrors*, the murderess seems like an interbellum ideal of the unworldly, frail woman whom men, and women, want to protect, but her unworldliness is shown as culpable complicity with wrong-doing and her frailty is also revealed as a kind of strength which means she survives where others don't.

Miss Marple herself is the chief vehicle of such ironic play, constantly revealing the superiority of the (female) amateur sleuth over the (male) professionals, or, indeed, over men in general:

'I understand that picric acid explodes if you drop a weight on it, and you will remember, dear vicar, that you met Mr Redding carrying a large stone just in the part of the wood where you picked up that crystal later. Gentlemen are so clever at arranging things – the stone suspended above the crystals and then a time fuse – or do I mean a slow match?'

(*MV*: ch. 30)

Needless to say, the vicar has not remembered the stone and he, along with the other men in the novel with the exception of the criminal, is not clever at arranging things. The cliché about men's practical abilities is given with a little spinsterly flutter which alerts the reader to an enjoyable recognition of its absurdity. In such details of dialogue and plot situation, Christie's detective novels are shrewdly critical and subversive of the social structures their overall ideology undoubtedly sustains.

Perhaps the greatest irony of all concerns the popularity of the Marple novels. These hugely successful stories, which have earned the Christie estate vast sums of money and are regarded affectionately by thousands of readers and, since their televised versions, by thousands of viewers, represent the detective novel at its most domestic and humble. As we shall see in Chapters Two and Three, Christie achieved this grand democratization of the genre by exploiting prejudices against women (that their lives are trivial) and against the old (that they are foolish and tiresome). For what the Miss Marple novels propose is that there is a logic which is structured around the minutiae of life which can nevertheless inexorably reach into the very depths of human society and the human psyche. And they suggest that women, particularly old women, because they are attuned to the trivia of existence, are therefore endowed with logical powers which make them ideal arbiters of justice and, indeed, instruments of Fate:

'You know, Raymond, my dear [said Miss Marple], if *I* were producing [*Macbeth*] I would make the three witches *quite* different. I would have them three ordinary, normal old women. Old Scottish women. They wouldn't dance or caper. They would look at each other rather slyly and you would feel a sort of menace just behind the ordinariness of them.'

(*SM*: ch. 8)

Chapter Two

MISS MARPLE THE SPINSTER

'**D**EAR OLD tabbies are the only possible right kind of female detective and Miss M is lovely', wrote Dorothy L. Sayers to Agatha Christie, soon after the publication of the first Miss Marple book, The Murder at the Vicarage, in 1931. That same year, Sayers had introduced her own tabbies, women 'of the class unkindly known as "superfluous" ' who belong to the Cattery, the detective agency set up by Lord Peter Wimsey in Strong Poison. Most of the Cattery's superfluous women are spinsters and it is Wimsey's charity as well as his shrewdness which fills their vacant hours and their empty purses by providing them with work in the field of crime detection. The head of the Cattery is Miss Climpson who, like Miss Marple, specializes in gossip as the means to the discovery of the criminal.

If women detectives had been present in fiction since the 1860s, the advent of the elderly spinster detective is a later development, her first appearance, according to Michele B. Slung, being Miss Amelia Butterworth, the 'meddlesome old maid' in Anna K. Green's *The Affair Next Door* (1897) (Slung, 1976: xxii). But this was an American novel and it seems that as far as the English detective novel was concerned the elderly spinster had to wait for the 1920s when Christie saw the potential of such a character in the figure of Miss Sheppard, the doctor's sister, in *The Murder of Roger Ackroyd*: 'She had been my favourite character in the book – an acidulated spinster, full of curiosity, knowing everything, hearing everything: the complete detective service in the home' (*Auto*: 448). Dr Sheppard regards his sister with affectionate contempt as a gossip and busybody but Hercule Poirot acknowledges her power and usefulness as a collector of information and an intuitive discoverer of the truth: 'Women observe subconsciously a thousand little details, without knowing that they are doing so. Their subconscious mind adds these little things together – and they call the result intuition' (*MRA*: ch. 13).

It is worth comparing Miss Sheppard's kind of detective ability, which is in embryo Miss Marple's ability to accumulate the trivial details of ordinary life and discover relationships between them which lead to the truth of the crime, with the detective prowess of the only other elderly spinster detective of 1920s fiction, Patricia Wentworth's Miss Maud Silver. At first Miss Silver seems to share spinsterish qualities in common with Miss Marple and to be very much her precursor. Like Miss Marple, Miss Silver admires Tennyson and is in other ways old-fashioned; in particular, she is a dedicated knitter: 'What a Victorian little person! [Charles] became aware of a half-knitted stocking on her lap, still needles bristling . . . . She picked up the stocking and began to knit, holding the needles in the German way' (*The Grey Mask* (1929): ch. 11). But in her detection Miss Silver has none of the credibility of Miss Sheppard or Miss Marple; in quite impossible ways Miss Silver appears at the scene of a potential crime, guesses who is the murderer without explanation or rationale, and generally seems to belong more to the crude thriller than to the detective story of logic and deduction which was reaching its zenith during this inter-war period. Her spinsterish appearance is inconsistent with her sensational behaviour and also with the far-fetched plots of the novels she features in. By contrast, the character of Miss Marple has a stereotypical realism which is sufficiently convincing to suspend our disbelief for the duration of the stories; she is what we believe an elderly spinster should be and her detective methods derive from these characteristics. The setting of the Marple stories, and their plot strategies, are likewise appropriate to the lifestyle of an elderly spinster. It is possible, however, that as an avid reader of detective stories Christie knew Wentworth's work, was struck by the idea of such a detective, and borrowed some of Miss Silver's features, particularly the knitting habit, when she came to develop her own spinster detective the year after *The Grey Mask* was published.

Before Miss Marple's actual advent, however, the spinster in Christie's work makes a further and rather shadowy appearance in a Poirot novel published in 1928, *The Mystery of the Blue Train*, in which St Mary Mead, the village in Kent where Miss Marple will eventually be found to be living, is first mentioned. An inferior work which Christie always disliked, *The Mystery of the Blue Train* was the first novel to be written after the breakdown of her marriage to Archie Christie and was wrung out of her by financial necessity. She claimed that it was the book that changed her from an amateur into a professional, which meant writing 'even when you don't want to, don't much like what you are writing, and aren't writing particularly well' (*Auto*. 369).

The rather nondescript, unmarried heroine of *The Blue Train* has lived for ten years in St Mary Mead as the companion to a Mrs Harfield who at the beginning of the novel has died, leaving Katherine a legacy. Amidst the foreign adventures this money enables her to have, including a murder investigation, Katherine often thinks nostalgically of the stability and ordinariness of St Mary Mead and at one point returns there to nurse an elderly friend, a spirited spinster of the Miss Sheppard type. At the end of the novel Katherine makes an unlikely marriage to a charming and irresponsible man and thus avoids the fate that has seemed to be her destiny, that of becoming a respectable spinster herself. It is difficult not to see an element of autobiographical wishful-thinking in this ending in which Christie's own probable 'spinster' future as a divorced woman is rejected for a romanticized solution in which a wayward man sees the folly of his ways and cleaves to a sensible, mature woman. It also provides the romantic interest which at that time Christie believed was a necessary ingredient in a detective story but which she later largely rejected as digressive.

Christie's dwelling on her broken marriage emerged most forcefully in the Mary Westmacott novels she began to write around the same time as she initiated the Miss Marple novels. In libraries these Mary Westmacott novels, of which six were published between 1930 and 1956, are usually classified as romantic fiction. They are not, however, love-and-marriage stories of a Barbara Cartland type but are the fictional workings-out of experiences and anxieties from Christie's own life. In particular, *Unfinished Portrait* (1934) is a highly autobiographical account of a girl's happy childhood, her marriage to a selfish, charming man, and her suicidal reaction to the death of her much-loved mother and her husband's desertion of her and their daughter. In her *Autobiography* Christie said that the period in which such events took place in her own life (1926–7) was one which 'I hate recalling' (*Auto*: 356), yet she did recall it, in considerable detail, in this novel published pseudonymously eight years afterwards. The heroine of *Unfinished Portrait* is left at the end of the novel with an uncertain future; no longer suicidal but alone and with her daughter having married, there is no easy Romance solution offered to her but merely the assumption that she will go 'back into the world to begin a new life'. By this time Christie herself had remarried but the anxieties concerning a woman left without the love and protection of a man stayed with her for a long time and were the fertile ground from which sprang Miss Marple, who will demonstrate that a man-less existence is not without its excitements and usefulness, and even its power.

In becoming a divorced woman, Christie tacitly joined the ranks of 'surplus women' whose presence in the population had been an issue since the middle years of the nineteenth century. By 1911 there were 1.3 million more women than men in England and Wales, increasing to 1.7 million by the time of the 1921 census and remaining at this level until well into the 1930s when equalization of emigration amongst men and women began to adjust the population balance between the sexes. But when Christie began writing of Miss Marple in the late 1920s, of every thousand persons in the population 43 were spinsters or widows (Adam, 1975: 85) and doomed to remain so; there were simply not enough men to go round. In the nineteenth century the 'redundant women' had generally been regarded as a pathetic embarrassment but by the 1920s their situation, although still often a source of derision, had also come to seem interesting and even slightly sinister. 'Too many women in this part of the world', says Colonel Melchett (*MV*: ch. 7) and he associates this surplus with disorder in the life of the village. Fear of the unmarried woman, and an accompanying misogyny, was partly a legacy from the First World War in which women had been encouraged to be economically independent and to take on jobs that hitherto had been regarded as suitable only for men. The war had also left complex attitudes of guilt and resentment as far as women, particularly spinsters, were concerned: so many men dead, so many women leading apparently useless, or at least sterile, and therefore unjustified lives. Moreover, the decade following the war had seen legislation which seemed to grant women political and employment opportunities hitherto undreamed of. Although much of this legislation bore little practical fruit, the very sound of it – the Parliament (Qualification of Women) Act of 1918 and the Sex Disqualification (Removal) Act of 1919, for example – produced anxious and retrograde reactions from a whole range of institutions and individuals from the Civil Service to the TUC, from D.H. Lawrence to Lloyd George. Yet in spite of opposition and continuing discrimination, this was, as Ruth Adam says, 'the era of the spinster. At last, after so many years of being grudged the right to exist at all, she came into her own' (Adam, 1975: 100).

The fate of the single woman had been a major theme in the Victorian novel from Elizabeth Sewell's *The Experience of Life* (1853) to George Gissing's *The Odd Woman* (1893). In the post-war era it seems to have become more prominent and also more variously treated. The range of attitudes it encompassed in this period can be seen in four novels of the 1920s: *Life and Death of Harriett Frean* (1922) by May Sinclair, *The Unlit Lamp* (1924) by Radclyffe Hall, *The Crowded Street* (1924) by Winifred Holtby, and *Lolly Willowes* (1926) by Sylvia Townsend Warner.

May Sinclair, who was influenced by Freudian psychology, suggests in *Life and Death of Harriett Frean* that spinsterhood is the inevitable outcome of the repressed sexuality of the 'good' middle-class girl whose niceness is guaranteed by sexual ignorance and hypocrisy. Harriett has the opportunity to marry but the sacrificial life of a dutiful daughter at home fulfils her repressive conditioning more than marriage could do. In Sinclair's devastatingly single-minded and schematic portrayal of this kind of spinster life, Harriett dies of a cancer which she believes is a baby, imagining herself also to be a baby, returning literally to the infantilism that has dominated her life.

Sinclair's other novel of a dutiful daughter, *Mary Olivier* (1919), resembles in some respects Radclyffe Hall's *The Unlit Lamp* in that the heroines of both novels are the victims of frailly tyrannical widowed mothers. But Mary Olivier makes her servitude into a triumph of self-education (she is the reverse mirror image of Harriett Frean) whereas Radclyffe Hall's heroine, Joan Ogden, 'large-boned . . . lanky as a boy', succumbs to a dreary routine of caring for her selfish mother, abandoning her career, and her passionate friendship for another woman, to do so. The novel makes clear that it is not just the power of the mother which is to blame but also a timidity in the daughter which causes her to cling, rebelliously but also with relief, to ideals of sacrificial femininity.

Winifred Holtby's *The Crowded Street* takes a more positive view of the spinster's role in society. Its heroine, Muriel, wastes her youth waiting to be married but when eventually the chance of marriage comes, she no longer wants it. Holtby's novel transmutes the loneliness and humiliation of Muriel's life into something of a feminist statement of independence, personhood and dedication to an ideal wider than the domestic. This is valiant and progressive spinsterhood:

> 'I've got an idea . . . an idea of service – not just vague and sentimental, but translated into quite practical things. Maybe I'll do nothing with it, but I do know this, that if I married you I'd have to give up every new thing that has made me a person . . . . I can't be a good wife until I've learnt to be a person . . . and perhaps in the end I'll never be a wife at all.'
>
> (*The Crowded Street* ch. 39)

More inventive than any of these three novels, and possessed of a bitter gaiety and whimsy, *Lolly Willowes* turns to paganism to solve the problems of its heroine who breaks free of her protected dependency with her brother and his family to live in the countryside, to become a benevolent witch, and to have intercourse with the Devil. As Lolly says, women like her are driven to these extremes in order 'to have a life of one's own, not an existence doled out to you by others, charitable refuse of their thoughts, so many ounces of stale bread of life a day'.

Christie's creation of Miss Marple must be seen against this background of social and literary concern with the spinster. Indeed, the whole range of Christie's detective fiction shows an astute awareness of the circumstances and range of spinster life and she includes many unmarried women in her novels apart from Miss Marple herself. *A Murder is Announced* (1950), for example, is particularly rich in single women and the very substance of the plot and the cause of the crime depend on their interaction. There are, to begin with, two spinster couples: Miss Blacklock and Miss Bunner who live together at Little Paddocks, and Miss Hinchliffe and Miss Murgatroyd who live at Boulders. These women are around 60 years old, and since the novel is set in the late 1940s this means that they would have been of that generation of young women whose potential partners were killed in the First World War. Indeed, Miss Blacklock thinks of Miss Bunner as one of life's casualties because she has not been able to marry: 'She ought, her friend thought, to have married some nice Army officer, or a country solicitor . . . . She had had to earn her living. She had been painstaking but never competent'. Miss Blacklock's own youth had also been thwarted, in her case by a disfiguring goitre left untreated by her obstinate, narrow-minded father. But Miss Blacklock is, of course, not the Miss (Letitia) Blacklock she pretends to be but her sister, Charlotte. It is on the substitution of one sister for the other that the murder plot hangs, and the substitution comes about because Charlotte Blacklock wants to recompense her years as an impoverished, invalid spinster by means of the money her sister is destined to inherit. But her sister Letitia (Letty) dies prematurely and so Charlotte (Lotty) begins her life of impersonation and deception, safe but for the tiresome, needy, affectionate Dora Bunner who had known both sisters in their childhood, who therefore has to be allowed to share the secret and its benefits and who eventually is murdered because of her knowledge. The bond between Miss Blacklock and Dora Bunner has its origins in their shared desire to escape the poverty and limitations of spinster life; it is a guilty bond and ultimately a destructive one but Christie strikes a sympathetic note when she has Miss Blacklock grieve for the woman who has been murdered: 'it's Dora I mind about – after Dora was dead, I was all alone – ever since she died – I've been alone'.

The two Miss Blacklocks, Letitia and Charlotte, represent opposing and stereotyped images of the spinster common during the inter-war period: the de-sexed career woman and the frustrated wife and mother. Letitia trained as a chartered accountant, and had 'really got a man's mind . . . . I don't believe she was ever in love with any man . . . . She never knew any of the fun of being a woman', says the very feminine Mrs Goedler. But Charlotte did know the fun of being a woman – 'a pretty light-hearted affectionate girl' – and it is this thwarted femininity and reluctant spinsterhood which leads to disaster.

Miss Hinchliffe and Miss Murgatroyd apparently live together because of mutual affection. They are presented as a slightly stagey lesbian couple who address each other as Hinch and Murgatroyd, with Hinch, who has 'short man-like' hair and wears corduroy slacks and battledress tunic, taking male control over the foolish, amiable Murgatroyd. The couple descend from Radclyffe Hall's *The Well of Loneliness* (1928) but Christie shows them content in their relationship and tolerated by their village society. Unlike Stephen in Radclyffe Hall's novel, they are not racked by guilt and ostracism and their tragedy is the simple one of death from knowing too much and from playing the detective game with insufficient caution.

In the midst of these and other single women of less importance in the novel, Miss Marple reigns as spinster supreme; if they are versions of the idea, she is the idea itself. In appearance, age, manners, social class, she is the essence of the English spinster, certainly the English literary spinster who can trace her lineage back to Miss Bates in Jane Austen's *Emma*, Betsy Trotwood in Dickens's *David Copperfield*, the Amazon ladies of Elizabeth Gaskell's *Cranford*, and can perhaps nod in recognition to

Oscar Wilde's Miss Prism in *The Importance of Being Earnest* or
E.M. Forster's Charlotte Bartlett in *A Room with a View*. These are
all comic and benign characters, but it is not difficult to trace a
connection between them and the grotesque and threatening
images of the unmarried woman that prevail in popular
entertainment: the ugly sisters, the pantomime dame, the witch
in the gingerbread house. Sheila Jeffreys suggests that prejudice
against unmarried women, always present in society, gained a
new virulence during the early years of this century and in the
post-war period. Jeffreys cites the spinster-baiting magazine the
Freewoman which began its assault in the first issue with an article
entitled 'The Spinster' written 'By One':

> I write of the High Priestess of Society. Not of the mother of
> sons, but of her barren sister, the withered tree, the acidulous
> vessel under whose pale shadow we chill and whiten, of the
> Spinster I write. Because of her power and dominion. She,
> unobtrusive, meek, soft-footed, silent, shamefaced, bloodless
> and boneless, thinned to spirit, enters the secret recesses of the
> mind, sits at the secret springs of action, and moulds and
> fashions our emasculate society. She is our social nemesis.
> (*Freewoman*, November 1911, quoted in Jeffreys, 1985: 95)

Although cast in a largely comic and popular mode, Christie's
Miss Marple evokes and makes use of many of the disturbing
emotions that the spinster figure inspires: condescension and
scorn, of course, but also various kinds of fear. The spinster is
moral arbiter, curb of license and disorder, and image of repres-
sion; she is also what lies outside the normal expectations of a
woman's life as it is lived in patriarchal society and although this
diminishes her it also gives her the power of the abnormal over
the normal, to threaten, to judge, to undermine and to destroy.
It is Christie's harnessing of the spinster's potential as both
fearsome oddity and moral force to the structures and conventions of detective fiction that makes the Marple stories such
satisfying examples of the genre. As we shall see, Miss Marple
not only solves the crime in ways peculiar to the spinster but she
also comes to wield a power of an almost supernatural nature

which far surpasses Lolly Willowes's paganism. She becomes, as the writer in the *Freewoman* forewarned, a social Nemesis.

Like any figure out of folklore, Miss Marple arrives on the fictional scene fully developed, a perennial feature of the pastoral scene we are given in St Mary Mead, a scene which is to be shattered, albeit temporarily, by the murder. We are given very little information about her on her first appearance in *The Murder at the Vicarage*. It is only as more novels follow, and Miss Marple begins to engage Christie's affection (she was to like her far better than Poirot), that the character is given more depth. It then becomes possible to trace her biography from the clues Christie cannot resist leaving; although gaps remain, they can be filled by processes Miss Marple herself would have approved of – the accumulation of detail and the use of analogy.

We first hear of Miss Marple from Griselda, the vicar's young wife in *The Murder at the Vicarage*, who says she is 'the worst cat in the village'. The label of 'cat' or 'old pussy' continues to be used of her, in tones ranging from affection and respect to irritation and scorn, throughout the novels, particularly by police officers of senior rank. It denotes an interest in, indeed an obsession with, gossip and with the minutiae of neighbourhood life. It also denotes malice and perhaps has associations of witchcraft rather in the manner that the *Freewoman* writer thinks of the spinster's sinister witch-like practices as feline – 'soft-footed, silent'. But Miss Marple is not malicious or sinister and, as yet, there is no suggestion of any quality in the least out of the ordinary; for although, as Griselda says, Miss Marple 'always knows every single thing that happens – and draws the worst inferences from it', her omniscience is gained by careful observation and there is never any question of her using her information to harm the innocent or gratuitously wound anyone, unlike the other 'cats' in the village, Mrs Price Ridley, Miss Wetherby and Miss Hartnell. In fact, Miss Marple talks about people very little but she listens to what is said by and about them and if she draws adverse inferences from what is said, she keeps her counsel until the pursuit of justice impels her to speak.

Miss Marple is also introduced in *The Murder at the Vicarage* as 'a white-haired old lady with a gentle, appealing manner'. She was therefore 'born', as Christie tells us, 'at the age of sixty-five to seventy, which . . . proved most unfortunate, because she was going to have to last a long time in my life' (*Auto*: 450). It also means that she would have been a little girl during the 1860s, a teenager during the 1870s and fully grown during the last twenty years of the Victorian age. By the time of her last published appearance, in *Sleeping Murder* (1976), Jane Marple would be well over 100. But of course, in the world of Marple novels, although there is often a recognition that change does take place, Miss Marple herself changes very little, so that in *Nemesis* she familiarly appears as a fussy, slightly rheumaticky, elderly lady, hardly less frail than she had been forty years before in *The Murder at the Vicarage*, who thinks of herself in terms we have grown accustomed to: ' "An old pussy," said Miss Marple to herself. "Yes, I can see I'm quite recognizable as an old pussy. There are so many old pussies, and they are all so much alike." ' In the intervening novels there are some indications that Miss Marple is ageing and fading, and even that a particular case may be her last one. In *A Murder is Announced* (1950), she 'seemed indeed very old' and in *4.50 from Paddington* (1957) she is described as 'an elderly frail old lady', who has to employ her previous nurse, Lucy Eylesbarrow, to do the sleuthing for her. In *The Mirror Crack'd from Side to Side* (1962), Miss Marple is too weak to do her own gardening, having had a sufficiently severe attack of bronchitis to require a live-in companion for a while, paid for, as is usually the case with these extra services, by her nephew Raymond West. Dr Haydock, the same Dr Haydock who as a middle-aged man had presided in *The Murder at the Vicarage* thirty-two years before, recommends 'a nice juicy murder' as a tonic for Miss Marple in *The Mirror Crack'd from Side to Side*, a remedy he also advises for the after-effects of 'flu in the short story "The Case of the Caretaker' (*MMFC*). But in the last two novels, *At Bertram's Hotel* and *Nemesis*, Miss Marple has regained her health, although Christie cannot resist a joke at Miss Marple's and the reader's expense by having Lady Selena Hazy say, ' "Why I do believe that's old Jane Marple. Thought she was dead years ago. Looks a hundred." ' However old she looks, Miss Marple in these final novels is as youthful-elderly as she ever was; in fact, in *Nemesis* she is particularly sprightly and energetic and it is one of the few novels in which she allows herself to be placed in physical danger. Her admissions of fatigue and weakness in this novel, and her absent-mindedness, are ruses to gain information.

Apart from being told that she is white-haired and has a fussy but appealing and gentle manner, and that she flushes easily from excitement or embarrassment, we are not given details of Miss Marple's appearance in the first of her novels. It is in *The Thirteen Problems* (1932, but actually written before *The Murder at the Vicarage*), the collection of short stories, that she begins to assume a sharper outline. Appropriately, she looks like a Victorian; indeed her appearance is rather like that of the widowed Queen Victoria in woodcuts from the 1890s (Bott and Clephane, 1932: 43):

> Miss Marple wore a black brocade dress, very much pinched in round the waist. Mechlin lace was arranged in a cascade down the front of the bodice. She had on black lace mittens, and a black lace cap surmounted the piled-up masses of her snowy hair. Her faded blue eyes benignant and kindly, surveyed her nephew and her nephew's guests with gentle pleasure.
> (*TP*. 'The Tuesday Night Club')

At Mrs Bantry's dinner-party in the same collection of short stories Miss Marple is again portrayed as wearing black lace mittens and lace round her shoulders and over her hair. By the time of *A Pocketful of Rye* (1953) she has shed her Victorian garments for clothes which are vaguely Edwardian: 'an old-fashioned tweed coat and skirt, a couple of scarves and a small felt hat with a bird's wing'. In *Nemesis* (1971), this has again been slightly up-dated to inter-war clothing of 'a light tweed suit, a string of pearls and a small velvet toque'. Although they change, Miss Marple's clothes are always out of date, as one would expect of an elderly spinster lady of limited means who is, it is repeatedly stressed, very much a lady and therefore not likely to dress cheaply or flashily: 'an aged but good-quality suitcase reposed by her feet. [Inspector] Crump recognized a lady when he saw one.' This image of a 1930s old lady, of neat, tweed-wearing, frugal gentility, is the one that Joan Hickson has so successfully projected in the recent BBC television adaptations of the novels.

Miss Marple's spinster image is enhanced by the knitting she seems always to be engaged upon. She appears to knit for babies and one wonders whose babies these are. In *The Mirror Crack'd from Side to Side* it is explained that it is for the offspring of the 'nice little maids' whom she has employed in the past that Miss Marple makes 'all the little woolly coats', and in *Nemesis* there is the suggestion that she sends off parcels of woollen garments to charitable institutions. But to ask for whom Miss Marple knits is to miss the point of knitting as the sign of her spinster status and the metaphor of her detecting activity. As a motif, however, Christie took some time to realize its potential. Miss Marple does not knit in the first novel, *The Murder at the Vicarage*, but in the short story 'The Tuesday Night Club' (1932), where we meet her in her own home, she is knitting 'something white and soft and fleecy' (*TP*). The knitting has disappeared in *The Body in the Library* but it is present in a novel of the same year, *The Moving Finger*, and in the next one, *A Murder is Announced*, where she is described as 'heavily enmeshed in fleecy wool . . . that she was knitting and which turned out to be a baby's shawl'. The image of Miss Marple surrounded by fluffy wool reflects, of course, her fluffy appearance and manner but at the same time it suggests that she is surrounded by a cloud, like a Divinity, an image developed in *Nemesis* when Mr Rafiel, from beyond the grave, writes that 'I see you . . . in a cloud of pink wool.' The fact that she knits for babies signals her as protector of the innocent as well as the one who ravels together the threads of the crime. And, as we shall see in Chapter Three, by the time of her last novel, the aptly named *Nemesis*, the full significance of knitting as Miss Marple's insignia emerges as she takes on some of the powers of Fate itself, and knits the destinies of men and women.

Miss Marple's other practical activity is gardening. Like knitting it seems an appropriate occupation for a spinster lady living in a village but also like knitting it is an aid to detection;

knitting disarms and soothes people so that they are more
confiding, and gardening allows excellent opportunity for
snooping. In *The Murder at the Vicarage* Miss Marple's garden is
strategically placed (most editions of the novel include a plan of
the village which shows just how well-placed Miss Marple's
garden is) for observing a good deal of what happens in St Mary
Mead, particularly who comes and goes to the vicarage. More
than this, Miss Marple's gardening in this novel provides her
with a vital clue to the murderer's identity because in trying to
dispose of incriminating evidence he brings her 'the wrong sort
of stone for my rock gardens! And that put me on the right
track!' Also like knitting, gardening becomes a metaphor for
Miss Marple's detective role; attractive and useful plants are
encouraged and the weeds are kept down, and so it is with
human beings.

Like many a heroine before her, Miss Marple is without
family, with the exception of her nephew Raymond West and,
after *The Thirteen Problems*, (where they become engaged and
where she is called Joyce) his wife Joan. In *4.50 from Paddington*
(1957 and therefore twenty-seven years after Raymond West is
first mentioned) there is a great-nephew, David West,
Raymond's second son who works for British Rail, but his introduction into this Marple novel is no more than an expedient
to help Miss Marple solve a train murder. Raymond West, who
writes gloomy, modernist and very successful novels, and his
wife who paints what she likes to think are modern pictures –
'mostly jugs of dying flowers and broken combs on windowsills',
is Miss Marple's description – serve as a sophisticated, urban foil
to Miss Marple's apparent naivety 'bound up in this idyllic rural
life'. They are also the means by which Miss Marple can pursue
her occupation elsewhere than in St Mary Mead, having a large
income and a willingness to provide holidays for their aunt. In
A Murder is Announced Raymond has paid for Miss Marple to stay
at the Royal Spa Hotel in Medenham Wells, nicely on hand for
the murders that are to occur in the village of Little Cleghorn,
and in *At Bertram's Hotel* Raymond and Joan pay for Miss
Marple's stay at that expensive and bogus place. Of course, Miss

Marple's visit to the West Indies in *A Caribbean Mystery* is financed by Raymond – 'Why he should take so much trouble about his old aunt', Miss Marple wonders; 'possibly he was truly fond of her . . . in a slightly exasperated and contemptuous way' – to help her recover from a bout of pneumonia.

Raymond's bounty raises the question of Miss Marple's income, which is presumably a fixed income inherited from parents long since dead. She belongs to the group of ladies in St Mary Mead 'in reduced circumstances who lived in neat houses round the church, and who knew intimately all the ramifications of the county families even though they might not be strictly county themselves' (*PFR*: ch. 21). It is of the essence of her lady-like status that she does not work for her living, or that any work she does, including her detecting, is unpaid and is also not officially recognized. In *The Murder at the Vicarage*, for example, the obnoxious Inspector Slack takes the credit for the criminals being brought to justice: 'Naturally, nothing was said of Miss Marple's share in the business. She herself would have been horrified at the thought of such a thing.'

In many respects, Miss Marple's upbringing would have been very similar to that of the Madden sisters in George Gissing's *The Odd Women*. They too were young girls in the 1870s and their father, a doctor, believed wholeheartedly in the Ruskinian doctrine of women's separate sphere within the home 'which must be guarded against sordid cares to the last possible moment . . . women, old or young, should never have to think about money'. The Madden sisters had received instruction suitable to their breeding and the atmosphere of the house was intellectual:

> But it never occurred to Dr Madden that his daughters would do well to study with a professional object. In hours of melancholy he had of course dreaded the risks of life, and resolved, always with postponement, to make some practical provision for his family . . . . The thought, however, of his girls having to work for money was so utterly repulsive to him that he could never seriously dwell upon it.
>
> (*The Odd Women*: ch. 1)

Miss Marple's father must have made better provision for his daughter than Dr Madden managed to do for his poor girls whose efforts to survive are the pathetic theme of Gissing's novel. Even so, Miss Marple has to live carefully; rather than reducing her to an unsuitable marriage, to religiosity or to alcoholism, as happens with the Madden sisters, this genteel frugality sharpens Miss Marple's perceptions of people's behaviour and gives her an awareness of the financial pressures and temptations that assail them. In *A Murder is Announced* she notices a cheque she has written has been altered and this alerts her to the petty thieving of the murder victim and also suggests to her that this is inconsistent with him being a murderer, as everyone thinks:

> 'Some busy young married woman or some girl having a love affair – that's the kind who write cheques for all sorts of different sums and don't really look through their passbooks carefully. But an old woman who has to be careful of the pennies, and who has formed habits – that's quite the wrong person to choose. Seventeen pounds is a sum I *never* write a cheque for. Twenty pounds, a round sum, for the monthly wages and books. And as for my personal expenditure, I usually cash seven – it used to be five, but everything has gone up so . . . . Here's a personable young man – who filches a little bit here and a little bit there . . . all sorts of petty thefts [but] he'd *never* have done a thing like that – not for a moment! He wasn't that kind of person.'
>
> (*AMIA*: ch. 8)

In the same novel Miss Marple can sympathize with Dora Bunner's history of many years of '*shabbiness*. Darning one's clothes and hoping it won't show . . . . It's the *rent* – always the *rent* – that's *got* to be paid – otherwise you're out in the street.' Miss Marple is nowhere near as poor as Dora Bunner has been but she knows enough about the pinched life of spinsters to make her realize the gratitude Dora must feel to someone who makes her life comfortable, even if that gratitude includes condoning a fraud.

In spite of the genteel poverty of her old age, Miss Marple keeps a maid. It is possible to trace in the Marple novels the evolution of the female domestic servant from the 1920s to the 1970s and perceive through Christie's sketchy characterization something of a social revolution. In *The Murder at the Vicarage*, published in 1930 when there were 1.3 million domestic servants, the majority of whom were women (Dyhouse, 1989: 109), Miss Marple's maid is the faceless Emily, who cannot be trusted to air the beds properly for the visit of Raymond West. Perhaps Emily had been one of the 'nice little maids' whom Miss Marple recalls in *The Mirror Crack'd*: Amy, Clara, Alice and others who had come from St Faith's Orphanage to be trained by Miss Marple before going on to service elsewhere:

> Rather simple, some of them had been, and frequently adenoidal, and Amy distinctively moronic. They had gossiped and chattered with the other maids in the village and walked out with the fishmonger's assistant, or the under-gardener at the Hall, or one of Mr Barnes, the grocer's numerous assistants.
>
> (*MCFSS*: ch. 1)

It is one of these trainees from St Faith's Orphanage, Gladys Martin, who is killed in *A Pocketful of Rye*:

> 'Gladys came to me when she was seventeen and I taught her how to wait at table and keep the silver and everything like that. Of course she didn't stay long. They never do. As soon as she got a little experience, she went and took a job in a cafe. The girls nearly always want to do that. They think it's freer, you know, and a gayer life.'
>
> (*PFR*: ch. 13)

But at least Gladys, by the time this novel came to be written in 1953, has had a choice of employment, unlike 'my faithful Florence' whom Miss Marple recalls fondly in *4.50 from Paddington* and whose only alternative to domestic service seems to have been the care of aged parents until their deaths. Florence now (1957) takes in paying guests in Brockhampton, near enough to the scene of the crime for Miss Marple to stay with her and supervise the investigations carried out by Lucy Eylesbarrow.

The real change in domestic service is signalled in *The Mirror*

Crack'd from Side to Side (1962), where Miss Marple is looked after by Cherry who comes from the local housing estate, called the Development, and is 'one of the detachment of young wives who shopped at the supermarket and wheeled prams about the quiet streets of St Mary Mead'. Cherry does housework to help pay for Hire Purchase expenditure; she is cheerful and intelligent and although her washing-up leaves much to be desired, she is liked by Miss Marple and is still with her in the last written of the Marple novels, *Nemesis*. 'It was odd that nowadays it should be the educated girls who went in for all the domestic chores,' Miss Marple thinks: 'Students from abroad, girls *au pair*, university students in the vacation, young married women like Cherry Baker.'

It is made clear in *A Pocketful of Rye* that Miss Marple has been involved in the running of St Faith's Orphanage, obviously a church orphanage taking children whose parents had died or abandoned them. Such places were quite common until some years after the Second World War and prided themselves on placing their teenagers in respectable and unpresuming jobs – nursing or domestic work for the girls and a craft for the boys, or the army. Miss Marple's attitude to the orphanage is one of kindly condescension – 'We do our best for the girls there, try to give them a good training and all that.' As Robert Barnard says, servants in Christie's novels are frequently treated with contempt, particularly maidservants: 'The female domestic servant was among the most depressed classes of the time, yet Christie has no sympathy with her' (Barnard, 1980: 42). He attributes this to Christie's stereotypical and unromantic realism: 'In her experience kitchen-maids were ill-educated and inarticulate, so they are made such' (43). In the Marple stories there is perhaps a cosier relationship between mistress and maid than Barnard allows and Miss Marple is occasionally provoked into detective action by unjust treatment of maids; in 'The Case of the Perfect Maid' (*MMFC*), she defends Gladys – 'an impertinent girl and far too pleased with herself but really strictly honest' – against charges of dishonesty, and in *A Pocketful of Rye* she avenges the death of another Gladys. But these instances are there to illustrate Miss Marple's integrity and compassion rather than the lives and characters of the servants and, in general, the attitude is that of middle-class irritation and incomprehension at the stupidity and laxity of the working class: 'Six spiders webs on the cornice, Miss Marple noted. These girls never raised their heads! She was none the less too kind to say so.' Barnard's comment about Christie's realism is born out by the fact that it is only with the advent, in *The Mirror Crack'd* (1962), of the independent and intelligent Cherry, a product of post-war affluence and educational opportunities, that a relationship between Miss Marple and one of her employees is given any attention, and the 'maid's' social position at all delineated.

Who Miss Marple's parents were is never exactly divulged but the inference is that her father was a clergyman and that in general she belongs to a clerical family. In *They Do it with Mirrors* she recalls a visit to Florence as a 'pink and white English girl from a Cathedral Close' and there are references to an Uncle Thomas who was Canon of Ely and another uncle who had been Canon of Chichester Cathedral. Like most nineteenth-century girls of her class, she was educated by a governess, as she describes to Inspector Slack in 'The Case of the Perfect Maid' (*MMFC*):

> 'So difficult to explain oneself, don't you think? . . . you see, not having been educated in the modern style – just a governess, you know, who taught one the dates of the kings of England and general knowledge . . . . And how labels are made, and all that. Discursive, you know, but not teaching one to keep to the point.'

As we shall see, the discursive method that is the hallmark of Miss Marple's detective methods is superior to the single-mindedness of the rival detectives, particularly Inspector Slack. Also, 'how labels are made' is a nicely ironic remark because this apparently useless occupation is yet another of Miss Marple's detecting strengths: the classifying and labelling of people by analogy is what so often leads her unerringly to the criminal.

One can begin to conjecture Miss Marple's childhood from the glimpses the novels give: a large, slightly shabby rectory, an absent-minded clergyman father a little like Canon Penny-feather in *At Bertram's Hotel*, a strong-minded mother and grand-mother with whom she paid the occasional visit to Paris or London, an Aunt Helen, and also at least one sister – because although we never hear her mentioned there is the existence of nephew Raymond West. Miss Marple's early history has some of the shape and texture of Christie's own girlhood, so much loved and so rich a source for nostalgia.

This nostalgia is tapped most resonantly, and also exposed as a suspicious mixture of memory and deception, in *At Bertram's Hotel*. Chief-Inspector Davy is struck by the phoneyness of the place, and particularly by the old lady 'with white fluffy hair and the knitting . . . . Might almost be on the stage, mightn't she? Everybody's universal great-aunt.' Miss Marple is an 'authentic' great-aunt whereas most of the other old-world characters are not what they seem. The detective plot involves the unmasking of these figures to reveal the robbers and cheats they actually are. It is an irony that the most anachronistic and nostalgic of all the characters in the novel, Miss Marple, is the means by which this exposure is effected: the myth dismantling itself. But whilst the double exposure unfolds, the reader is treated to a reminiscence, or a fantasy, of what a good hotel used to be like, and, by extension, of a lost and desired world of dignified wealth, comfortable life-styles and good things to eat, par-ticularly nursery-type food like muffins. At one point in the novel Miss Marple goes on a sentimental tour of London, visit-ing the shops, gardens and squares she used to visit as a girl, noting the changes that have occurred: flats in what used to be family houses and a vast skyscraper of modernistic design (the year is 1965) in Lowndes Square where Lady Merridew, a distant cousin, had once lived in some style. It is a sentimental trip for the reader also, or particularly those readers who could look back with fond regret to the pre-war days when a comfortably-off middle-class woman like Miss Marple's Aunt Helen, could spend an hour in the Army and Navy Stores with her special assistant in the grocery department, 'thinking of every conceivable grocery that could be purchased and stored up for future use'.

But it was a constricting world also, particularly for a genteely reared girl like Jane Marple. Whilst Aunt Helen made her purchases, the young Jane fidgeted and was told to 'go and look at the glass department by way of amusement'. Girls during this period had to be content with very little in the way of amusement. 'My father's slogan was that boys should go everywhere and know everything, and that a girl should stay at home and know nothing', wrote M.V. Hughes in *A London Child of the 1870s* (Hughes 1977). If this was a general attitude – and Hughes's account describes her childhood as being more than usually happy – looking at the glass department could well be seen as an exciting occupation for a girl.

The occasional glimpses of a once lively girl, whose experiences were very much based on Christie's own with her mother and Auntie-Granny, evaporate as far as the young womanhood and middle years of Miss Marple are concerned. Whereas Christie married (twice), had a child, became a writer and an amateur archaeologist, travelled, and earned money and fame, Jane Marple entered a kind of shadow life about which we learn very little until she emerges as a detective in old age. 'I am used to sick people,' she says in *Nemesis*, 'I have had a good deal to do with them in my time', and from this remark we deduce a middle-age spent in caring for frail parents and perhaps other relatives also. We also hear from her of the loneliness of old age: 'I have nephews and nieces and kind friends – but there's no one who knew me as a young girl – no one who belongs to the old days. I've been alone for quite some time now' (*MIA*: ch. 17). Before the resignation of maturity, she must have spent many years, in however well-bred a manner, waiting for the right husband to turn up; even if she herself did not expect or want it, it would have been expected on her behalf. However comfortable in her single state, and eventually grateful for it, the ignominy of not marrying cannot entirely have escaped her, and the stigma of being an old maid must have clung to her as she grew past youth, just as it did to the heroine of Winifred Holtby's *The Crowded Street*.

She knew now what they thought of her, a thorough-going old maid, mean and spiteful. She saw herself with the eyes of those young girls beyond the door. She contrasted their gay, ruthless youth with her bitter maturity. She saw the ten wasted years that lay behind her, and her barren future. She saw herself, grown sour with disappointment, grudging to Delia her happiness, to Connie her liberty, fretting herself over tasks that others might have performed as well, and having to learn generosity from women whom she despised.

(*The Crowded Street*: ch. 24)

But by the time we meet Miss Marple she seems to have no regrets about the loss of marriage, gratefully recalling, in *At Bertram's Hotel*, how her mother had intervened in an unsuitable youthful affair:

Jane Marple, that pink and white eager young girl . . . . Such a silly girl in many ways . . . now who was that very unsuitable young man whose name – oh dear, she couldn't even remember it now! How wise her mother had been to nip that friendship so firmly in the bud. She had come across him years later – and really he was quite dreadful! At the time she had cried herself to sleep for at least a week.

(*ABH*: ch. 2)

Perhaps her apparent lack of regret at not having married has to do with her rather poor opinion of men. She is not above appreciating their masculinity – 'her candid blue eyes swept over the manly proportions and handsome face of Detective-Inspector Craddock with truly feminine Victorian appreciation . . . . Detective-Inspector Craddock blushed' – but otherwise she has sharp comments to make about 'gentlemen', as she refers to the opposite sex, 'as though it were a species of wild animal'. Usually her remarks are to the effect that men are childish and demanding: 'gentlemen are usually rather selfish . . . gentlemen so *easily* feel neglected', she says in *The Body in the Library*, and they are more emotional and illogical than they would like to believe, 'frequently not as level-headed as they seem'. And, as the novels repeatedly demonstrate, the logic of men, although, as Miss Marple says, it 'always seem[s] to be able to tabulate things so clearly', misses, or considers irrelevant, the really important facts. On moral grounds, also, men often seem to be lacking; they are tyrannical, like Colonel Protheroe in *The Murder at the Vicarage*, or possessive, like Dr Kennedy in *Sleeping Murder*, or simply a bore, like Major Palgrave in *A Caribbean Mystery*. Most of all, men are not really to be trusted; economically and sexually they have greater power than women and this makes them predatory and careless:

> 'Women have a much worse time of it in the world than men do. They're more vulnerable. They have children, and they mind – terribly – about their children. As soon as they lose their looks, the men they love don't love them any more. They're betrayed and deserted and pushed aside.'
>
> (*TDIWM*: ch. 16)

These words are spoken by a young woman, not Miss Marple, but they carry an unmistakable authorial weight; in conjunction with the many tart things Miss Marple has to say about men, they give an impression that perhaps it is not so bad to be unmarried, that spinsterhood is not without its attractions.

In the final Marple novel, *Nemesis*, when Miss Marple calls to collect her money after the successful solving of the murder mystery, she tells the solicitor that she is going to have fun spending it:

> She looked back from the door and she laughed. Just for one moment Mr Schuster . . . had a vague impression of a young and pretty girl shaking hands with the vicar at a garden party in the country. It was, as he realized a moment later, a recollection of his own youth. But Miss Marple had, for a minute, reminded him of that particular girl, young, happy, going to enjoy herself.
>
> (*N*: ch. 23)

The inference is that not only has Jane Marple been lively and attractive when young but that she still is young, that her life of spinsterhood has not dimmed her sparkle and that the energy which might have been spent in marriage is directed into other things, notably sleuthing, and that it is this single state and its activities which keep her young.

In this respect, Miss Marple, the spinster who withstands the processes of time, is rather like the village she lives in, St Mary Mead. Both seem to have a kind of mythic permanence which protects them from biological and social change. When St Mary Mead is first featured, in *The Murder at the Vicarage*, there is little verbal description but there is a map in which the conventional features of an English village are indicated: the church and vicarage, the doctor's house, the station, the Blue Boar, the Old Hall on the outskirts, and various cottages and small shops. Christie sticks to this basic formula in subsequent novels but, through Miss Marple, she registers a superficial change:

> St Mary Mead, the old world core of it, was still there. The Blue Boar was there, and the church and the vicarage and the little nest of Queen Anne and Georgian houses, of which hers was one . . . . But though the houses looked much as before, the same could hardly be said of the village street. When shops changed hands there, it was with a view to immediate and intemperate modernization.
>
> (*MCFSS*: ch. 1)

In *The Mirror Crack'd*, published in 1962, Miss Marple ponders such changes, particularly the Development, the new housing estate built beyond the vicarage where once Farmer Giles's cattle had grazed in meadows. 'And why not? Miss Marple asked herself sternly. These things had to be. The houses were necessary, and they were well built, or so she had been told.' This is an example of the way in which Christie causes Miss Marple to register the passage of time and the arrival of new ideas. In *A Murder is Announced* (1950), for instance, the cold War, the decline in the mining industry, psychological theories, war-widows, refugees, and land girls, are all mentioned, and in *At Bertram's Hotel* (1965) Miss Marple refers to both Marx and the Beatles. There is a patina of modernity to the stories which is self-consciously maintained. In *At Bertram's Hotel*, the penurious and well-named relic from earlier times, Lady Selina Hazy, describes St Mary Mead as a 'sweet unspoilt village . . . . Just the same as ever, I suppose?' But Miss Marple demurs and thinks of 'the additions to the Village Hall, the altered appearance of the High Street with its up-to-date shop fronts'. Yet it is only the shop fronts that change, and the Hall is added to, not removed; reassuringly the basic structures of village life remain the same, and likewise the people who live there:

> The new world was the same as the old. The houses were differ-
> ent, the streets were called Closes, the clothes were different, the
> voices were different, but the human beings were the same as
> they had always been. And though using slightly different
> phraseology, the subjects of conversation were the same.
>
> (*MCFSS*: ch. 2)

Like Miss Marple shedding her Victorian clothes, St Mary Mead changes its surface appearance, but fundamentally remains the same. Since St Mary Mead stands for the whole of society, the implication is that human society and human personality do not change either. In the conservative world of detective fiction, permanence and fixity are endorsed; change is superficial, disturbance is temporary, the murderer is discovered, and the characteristics of human beings can be classified by the wise and experienced individual. As we shall see in Chapter Three, Miss Marple the spinster is exactly that wise and experienced figure who presides over the unchanging vagaries of human nature. The final irony of this is that she is, of course, the protector of a society that despises her, or, at best, treats her with amused tolerance. Although in becoming a successful sleuth Miss Marple subverts the 'spinster' category by which society seeks to diminish and trivialize her, the role of the detective she assumes is, nevertheless, to protect and stabilize that society and its structures of patrilineal inheritance and property-ownership which have always borne most heavily against the single woman.

Chapter Three

TWO GILLS OF PICKED SHRIMPS: MISS MARPLE AS DETECTIVE

I N THE early collection of short stories, *The Thirteen Problems* (1932), a group of friends gather in Miss Marple's house and, after a few preliminaries, begin to tell each other of mysteries they have encountered. Of course, it is Miss Marple who provides the solution each time. The group calls itself the Tuesday Night Club and its members are the stalwarts of Miss Marple's world: Sir Henry Clithering, ex-Commissioner of Scotland Yard; Dr Pender, a clergyman; Mr Petherick, the solicitor; and Raymond West, Miss Marple's nephew, and his friend, later to be his wife, Joyce Lempriere. The group initially does not think to include Miss Marple in its detection games – 'I didn't think you would care to play', says Joyce – and there is also a certain amount of amusement towards her when she begins to offer an example of an unsolved mystery, the case of the missing shrimps:

> 'Mrs Carruthers had a very strange experience yesterday morning. She bought two gills of picked shrimps at Elliot's. She called at two other shops and when she got home she found she had not got the shrimps with her. She went back to the two shops she had visited but these shrimps had completely disappeared. Now that seems to me very remarkable.'
>
> 'A very fishy story,' said Sir Henry Clithering gravely.
>
> 'There are, of course, all kinds of possible explanations', said Miss Marple, her cheeks growing slightly pinker with excitement. 'For instance, somebody else –'
>
> 'My dear Aunt,' said Raymond West with some amusement, 'I

didn't mean that sort of village incident. I was thinking of murders and disappearances . . .'

(TP: 'Tuesday Night Club')

The picked shrimps (only one gill of them this time) are mentioned in the first Miss Marple novel, *The Murder at the Vicarage*, where Griselda says, 'I wish you'd solve the case, Miss Marple, like you did the time Miss Wetherby's gill of picked shrimps disappeared. And all because it reminded you of something quite different about a sack of coals' (ch. 11). The shrimps are also mentioned in a later novel, *Sleeping Murder*, where they have become pickled rather than picked, presumably because by 1976 (when the novel was published, although it was written in 1940) no one used the former term. In whatever state, the shrimps have become part of Miss Marple's personal mythology:

> 'She adores problems . . . . Any kind of problem. Why the grocer's wife took her umbrella to the church social on a fine evening. Why a gill of pickled shrimps was found where it was. What happened to the Vicar's surplice. All grist to my Aunt Jane's mill.'

(SM: ch. 3)

By this time, the shrimps have become the emblem of Miss Marple's method of detection in that they represent both the trivia of everyday life and its mysteries. They constitute the basic premiss of the Marple books which is that if one can solve the mystery of missing shrimps, one can also solve problems of much greater seriousness, including murder. Human nature is the same whether it is engaged upon stealing shrimps or plotting to kill another human being and St Mary Mead is, in its miniature way, as much a seat of evil (and goodness) as the busiest town, a truth that Miss Marple's friends, particularly her nephew Raymond, do not always appreciate. As Miss Marple says to him:

> 'You think that because I have lived in this out-of-the-way spot I am not likely to have had any very interesting experiences [but] human nature is much the same everywhere, and, of course, one has opportunities of observing it at close quarters in a village.'

(TP: 'The Thumb Mark of St Peter')

Indeed, it is only the bumptious and unthinking who dismiss St Mary Mead as unsuitable training ground for the student of human nature and therefore for the detective, as Miss Marple sharply points out to that 'rather exquisite young man', Raymond:

'I regard St Mary Mead,' he said authoritatively, 'as a stagnant pool.'

'That is really not a very good simile, dear Raymond,' said Miss Marple briskly. 'Nothing, I believe, is so full of life under the microscope as a drop of water from a stagnant pool.'

'Life – of a kind,' admitted the novelist.

'It's all much the same kind, really, isn't it?' said Miss Marple.
(*MV*: ch. 21)

The short stories in *The Thirteen Problems* represent Miss Marple's detecting methods at their most simple and they particularly illustrate the irrelevance of the environment to the central issue of the crime. Each story features a different speaker and creates its own atmosphere which at first seems to be of vital importance. 'The Idol House of Astarte' resembles a Gothic horror story, 'Ingots of Gold' a Cornish smuggling yarn, and 'The Bloodstained Pavement' is like a ghost story. In fact, atmosphere is shown to be a red herring which deceives the less logical and clear-sighted of the Tuesday Club members and provides temporary diversion for the clue-spotting reader. Miss Marple, however, like the good positivist thinker she is, can see beneath the paraphernalia of setting and atmosphere to the facts which lead to the crime. In 'The Bloodstained Pavement', what at first seemed like premonition was due to the murderer faking the time of the accident so that it appeared to happen earlier than it did, and in 'The Idol House of Astarte', a man apparently killed whilst no one is there is shown by Miss Marple as having tripped and knocked himself unconscious and been murdered by someone who comes to his rescue. The effect of such stories is, of course, to reassure the reader of the validity of human logic in the face of the uncanny; even when reality seems unreal and menacing, it is still subject to the laws of rationality.

Miss Marple, as a little old lady living in a village, is shown throughout as being the ideal detective. 'There's no detective in England equal to a spinster lady of uncertain age with plenty of time on her hands', says the vicar in *The Murder at the Vicarage*, and Sir Henry Clithering, via Inspector Craddock, describes Miss Marple as:

> 'just the finest detective God ever made – natural genius cultivated in a suitable soil. He told me never to despise the' – Dermot Craddock paused for a moment to seek for a synonym for 'old pussies' – 'elderly ladies. He said they could usually tell you what *might* have happened, what ought to have happened, and even what actually *did* happen! And . . . they can tell you *why* it happened. He added that this particular – er – elderly lady was at the top of the class.'
>
> *(FFP.* ch. 16)

The abilities old ladies possess – knowing what, how, and why something happened, and what ought to have happened – amount to the essential qualities of the detective: a strong moral sense, a knowledge of human nature, and a capacity for deduction based on carefully observed evidence. It is the 'trivial' lives of old ladies, who have plenty of leisure, the wisdom of experience, long memories, little personal drama in their own lives, and a huge capacity for vicarious living through observation of and gossip about the lives of others, that makes them into potentially excellent detectives. In *Gyn/Ecology* Mary Daly, (Daly, 1979: 75–9) notes that the term *trivia* was one of the names of the ancient triple goddess from whom Christian notions of the Trinity sprang; its modern meaning has been devalued into that which is slight, unimportant, commonplace, but its earlier meaning had to do with omnipresence, commonplace in the sense of being everywhere and facing in all directions. In the figure of Miss Marple Christie takes the patriarchal notion of the trivial and transforms it into something approaching its old meaning. The ordinary, gossipy, unsung life of an old lady is shown as a powerful force for good, and the full exercise of the womanly, highly personalized approach to society is portrayed in Miss Marple as necessary and life-saving. Agatha Christie was no obvious feminist, as she testifies in her

Autobiography, and in her novels she shows a deep dislike of career women, but she did give a high value to conventionally womanly attributes and habits and showed them, in the figure of Miss Marple, as the vehicles of logic, morality, and justice. In this respect Christie differs from many of her more obviously progressive contemporaries, for within her separate sphere Miss Marple is not only moral and caring – the traditional attributes of the good woman within patriarchy – but she is also an intellectual force, invading the male territories of logic and rationality. This makes her, as Inspector Craddock realizes, as 'dangerous as a rattlesnake'. Much of the pleasure of reading about Miss Marple, and watching her in the televised versions, stems from the contradiction involved in seeing a little old lady, a figure whom society in its ageism condemns as, at best, charmingly quaint and, at worst, as a tiresome nuisance, prove more inexorably logical than the most skilful policemen, and more depraved than the most ambitious evil-doer in the sense that, as Mrs Dane Calthrop says, she 'knows more about the different kinds of human wickedness than anyone I've ever known' (*MF*: ch. 14).

One of the chief attributes of Miss Marple, or reputedly so, is her capacity for gossip, stereotypically women's weakness, particularly if they are old and unmarried. Christie plays on this view of the elderly spinster and even on several occasions makes use of the negative image of the female village gossip:

> Miss Wetherby, a long-nosed, acidulated spinster, was the first to spread the intoxicating information. She dropped in upon her friend and neighbour Miss Hartnell.
> 'Forgive me coming so early, dear, but I thought, perhaps, you mightn't have heard the *news*.'
> 'What news?' demanded Miss Hartnell. She had a deep bass voice and visited the poor indefatigably, however hard they tried to avoid her ministrations.
>
> (*BL*: ch. 4)

And so the news of the body in Colonel Bantry's library is passed on and before long his implication in an unsavoury and murderous liaison is assumed:

'. . . I distinctly heard him tell the driver to go to – *where do you think?*'

Mr. Clement looked inquiring.

'An address in *St John's Wood*!'

Mrs. Price Ridley paused triumphantly.

The vicar remained completely unenlightened.

'That, I consider, *proves* it,' said Mrs. Price Ridley.

(*BL*: ch. 4)

Here, Mrs Price Ridley misinterprets the various pieces of information that have come her way. The body in Colonel Bantry's library, his reluctance to talk, the fact that St John's Wood was notoriously an area where men kept their mistresses, are placed in an erroneous relationship with each other resulting in a faulty 'proof'. Mrs Price Ridley is a bad detective as well as a bad gossip because her deductive powers are neither searching enough nor used with moral restraint. Miss Marple is a good gossip and therefore a good detective. She is no less interested in all scraps of information and would also have noted that Colonel Bantry took a taxi to St John's Wood. Equally she would have borne in mind that he was a man unlikely to keep a mistress and would have considered an alternative explanation for his going there. Above all, she would not have mentioned her speculations to anyone without much more assurance of the correctness and necessity of doing so. She is no idle gossip.

In a chapter appropriately called 'Miss Marple Comes to Tea' in *A Murder is Announced*, we see how Miss Marple uses gossip in a positive way. She appears to Letitia Blacklock as 'very charming in her gentle gossipy fashion' and seems to be one of those old ladies who have 'a constant preoccupation with burglars'. Since a murder has been committed in Miss Blacklock's house, this is a topic which seems both unsuspicious and inevitable; it also allows Miss Marple to ask probing questions and, more important, it prompts other characters to be indiscreet. The conversation winds in an apparently trivial and random manner towards the objectives Miss Marple has set for it, one of which is to discover if Miss Blacklock has known her nephew and niece as children. The issue is approached through a discussion of furniture.

> 'I must confess,' said Miss Marple, 'that my own few possessions are very dear to me, too – so many *memories*, you know. It's the same with photographs. People nowadays have so few photographs about. Now I like to keep all the pictures of my nephews and nieces as babies – and then as children – and so on.'
> 'You've got a horrible one of me, aged three,' said Bunch. 'Holding a fox terrier and squinting.'
> 'I expect your aunt has many photographs of you,' said Miss Marple, turning to Patrick.

At the right moment the question is asked, the information unsuspectingly given, and then it is stored away in Miss Marple's mind to be fitted into the puzzle at a later stage. It certainly is not squandered in idle speculation in the way of Mrs Price Ridley. In case the reader has missed the strategy Miss Marple employs, and with it a vital piece of information, the chapter concludes with a coda as follows:

> 'Did you do that on purpose?' said Bunch, as she and Miss Marple were walking home. 'Talk about photographs, I mean?'
> 'Well, my dear, it *is* interesting to know that Miss Blacklock didn't know either of her two young relatives by sight . . .'

The reader who thinks this is being spoon-fed in the way of clues, should be aware that other clues have been strewn around, one of them (the Letty/Lotty confusion) a clue of great importance which has been noted by Miss Marple (as we later learn) but not remarked upon:

> 'Oh, Letty,' exclaimed Miss Bunner. 'I forgot to tell you the Inspector was most peculiar this morning. He insisted on opening the second door – you know – the one that's never been opened – . . .'
> Too late she got Miss Blacklock's signal to be quiet, and paused open-mouthed.
> 'Oh, Lotty, I'm so – sorry – I mean, oh, I *do* beg your pardon Letty – oh, how stupid I am.'

Poor Dora Bunner, who is a silly rather than a malicious gossip, dies because she cannot control her tongue and also because she allows Miss Marple to exploit this tendency. Having morning coffee at the Bluebird Cafe they talk of rheumatism, sciatica, and neuritis and then progress to the poverty and loyalties of the past, Miss Blacklock's parasitical visitors whom Dora thinks are trying to kill her, and finally the substitution of one lamp for another. Amongst this plethora of unprocessed information, Miss Blacklock appears: 'Coffee and gossip, Bunny?', she ominously asks. As Miss Marple later says, 'I'm afraid that conversation with me in the cafe really sealed Dora's fate . . . . But I think it would have come to the same in the end . . . . Because life couldn't be safe for Charlotte while Dora Bunner was alive.' Like Mrs Price Ridley, Dora Bunner provides an example of gossip uncontrolled by rationality; from malice or from foolishness both characters misuse the information they possess and arrive at faulty conclusions, in Dora Bunner's case with fatal implications.

Christie's novels, like any detective novel, are full of false trails to test and beguile the reader and to enhance the eventual denouement and the prowess of the detective. In the small-village world of the Marple novels, what people hear and re-member of each other's conversations, and of their appearance and manner – the stuff of gossip – is the source of both truth and falsehood and the good detective has to thread her way amongst conflicting evidence to find the truth. There is never any doubt in Christie's novels that truth exists but there is awareness that people's apprehension of it, whether inten-tionally or not, is distorted. This is illustrated in the first murder scene of *A Murder is Announced* when the versions of what the gunman said vary according to the character, and detective reading habits, of the individuals involved, none of whom, as we later learn, has any reason at this point in the story to tell a lie. The feminine Miss Murgatroyd heard 'Put them up, please', while her more masculine friend says it was 'Stick 'em up!'; the romantic Mrs Swettenham heard 'Your money or your life', while Patrick Simmons opts for 'Stick your hands up', and his 'sister' Julia chooses 'Stick 'em up, guys.'

The important clues in this crucial scene in *A Murder is Announced*, which include a table-lamp, a vase of violets, and a door which has been closed off, are available to all to make sense of and most of the characters aim to do so but only some get anywhere near the truth, and only one, Miss Marple, actually reaches it. The parallel detecting plot which almost succeeds is that in which Hinchliffe forces Murgatroyd to remember the events of that first scene to which she applies Marple-like deductive powers. This amusing scene, in which Murgatroyd is instructed to 'use that fluff of yours you call a brain', is interrupted at the point of discovery by a telephone call asking Hinchliffe to collect a dog from the station. As she and Miss Marple later gaze at Murgatroyd's murdered body, Hinchliffe says, ' "My fault, in a way, that Murgatroyd's lying out there. I made a game of it . . . . Murder isn't a game." "No," said Miss Marple. "Murder isn't a game." ' Well, of course, in these books murder is a game but one that can only be successfully played by the very skilful gossip–detective, as the dialogue which follows the discovery of Murgatroyd's body illustrates. Hinchliffe is convinced by Murgatroyd's last words to her – 'She wasn't there' – that the murderer must have been one of three women, Mrs Swettenham, Mrs Easterbrook, and Julia Simmons. But Miss Marple points out that how one says things, where the emphasis falls, is very important, and when Hinchliffe admits that Murgatroyd said '*She* wasn't there', Miss Marple is able to make a reading of the clues which is superior to Miss Hinchliffe's. Playing the detective game is like life; if you get it wrong it can lead to death. And also if you allow the arbitrarinesses of life, like telephone calls summoning you to fetch dogs from stations, to interrupt the detective game, then that too can lead to death, and to your failure as a detective.

The Marple books are full of rival detectives, like the vicar and Raymond West in *The Murder at the Vicarage*, or Jerry Burton in *The Moving Finger*, and the schoolboys in *The Body in the Library* and *4.50 from Paddington*. The adult detectives are frequently foolish, jumping to premature conclusions, adducing half-baked psychological explanations (Raymond West is particularly prone to that) and not noticing things properly, but the schoolboys come off rather better and Christie has a soft spot for them. As the vicar says about his teenage nephew, at his age 'a detective story is one of the best things in life . . . . Death means very little to a boy of sixteen', and the enthusiasm and unfastidious curiosity of schoolboys make them into useful assistant sleuths. Young Peter Carmody in *The Body in the Library* finds and keeps a crucial finger-nail and the two boys in *4.50 from Paddington*, drawing on gloves 'in the best detective story tradition', produce an important envelope.

But of course the most active of those who conduct detective investigations parallel to Miss Marple's are the police; it is, after all, their job to solve the crime. Policemen range from those who collaborate with Miss Marple and respect and trust her, like Inspector Craddock and Sir Henry Clithering (who describes himself as Miss Marple's Watson) to the suspicious and truculent Inspector Slack who dislikes all women, and particularly that 'interfering old pussy', Miss Marple. Slack is a lugubrious version of the comic and inept policeman so dear to the hearts of classical detective readers and writers; his professionalism is gratifyingly shown to be less impressive than the prowess of the amateur sleuth. His great weakness is that he is not a gifted gossip; he does not know how to listen and he acts precipitately:

> Activity was always to Inspector Slack's taste. To rush off in a car, to silence rudely those people who were anxious to tell him things, to cut short conversations on the plea of urgent necessity. All this was the breath of life to Slack.
>
> (*BL*: ch. 3)

In *The Murder at the Vicarage* Inspector Slack constructs his solution on the basis of the immediate evidence of someone's confession: 'But there it was – a beautiful case. Mr Redding only too anxious to be hanged, so to speak.' As Miss Marple can show him, uncritically to accept what someone says is both gullible and lazy; although, as the vicar says, 'never did a man more determinedly strive to contradict his name,' Inspector Slack's name is appropriate because he is neither alert in listening to and decoding what people say nor strenuous in assembling all the relevant information. He happens in this case to be right –

Laurence Redding is an accomplice in the murder – but the plot has to take several more loops before this is revealed, bluff and double bluff, and it is not Slack who discovers the truth, even though he takes the credit for it.

The policemen who most successfully rival Miss Marple in the detecting business are those who most resemble her. This is the case with Chief-Inspector Fred Davy, in *At Bertram's Hotel*, who is known as Father:

> He had a comfortable spreading presence, and such a benign and kindly manner that many criminals had been disagreeably surprised to find him a less genial and gullible man than he had seemed to be.
>
> (*ABH*: ch. 4)

Father sits around, hums snatches of popular songs, is fond of muffins, and above all, unlike Slack, listens to what people have to say and indulges in a certain amount of speculative gossip. His is a wise passivity of a kind Miss Marple possesses, an ability to attract and then absorb and store diverse information and at the crucial point fit it together to solve the crime mystery:

> 'It's a funny thing, you know,' he went on, in a reminiscent, almost gossipy manner, looking like an old farmer discussing his stock and his land, 'I've learnt after a great many years' trial and error – I've learned to distrust a pattern when it's simple. Simple patterns are often too good to be true . . . actually behind the appearances, things might be rather different.'
>
> (*ABH*: ch. 26)

In this novel, the policeman is not a fool; although he may look or sound like one sometimes – large, fat, bovine-looking, buzzing like a bumble-bee – he is shrewd and logical, with a logic which admits into his analysis both the related and the impressionistic aspects of a situation. In this novel, Miss Marple acts as his confidante and aid rather than, as in, say, *A Murder is Announced*, the chief architect of detection. Yet she is finally right where he is wrong, not in the discovery of the crime syndicate Bess Sedgwick runs in Bertram's Hotel, which he successfully unmasks, but in sensing the evil that is brooding in the place, and in her premonition of the only murder that occurs in the novel:

> 'I'm glad to be leaving here,' said Miss Marple. She gave a little shiver. 'Before anything happens.'
> Chief-Inspector Davy looked at her curiously.
> 'What do you expect to happen?' he asked.
> 'Evil of some kind,' said Miss Marple.
> 'Evil is rather a big word – '
> 'You think it is too melodramatic? But I have some experience – seem to have been – so often – in contact with murder.'
> 'Murder?' Chief-Inspector Davy shook his head. 'I'm not suspecting murder. Just a nice cosy round up of some remarkably clever criminals –'
> 'That's not the same thing. Murder – the wish to do murder – is something quite different. It – how shall I say? – it defies God.'
> He looked at her and shook his head gently and reassuringly.
> 'There won't be any murders,' he said.
>
> (*ABH*: ch. 20)

Immediately Chief-Inspector Davy has said this, a murder occurs, committed, as it turns out, by someone who looks like 'one of the angels in an early primitive Italian painting' and for whom everyone has sympathy and believes innocent. In fact, there are two parallel criminal situations in this novel and Chief-Inspector Davy has too single-mindedly been concentrating on only one. Miss Marple's more 'trivial' approach has also registered the second, and more murderous, plot to do with a young girl's passion for an unscrupulous man who is also her mother's lover. Chief-Inspector Davy recognizes his own, and everyone else's, moral naivety compared with Miss Marple: 'Too many nice people who don't know anything about evil. Not like my old lady . . . . She's had a long life of experience in noticing evil, fancying evil, suspecting evil and going forth to do battle with evil' (*ABH*: ch. 22).

Such a comment, which reiterates what has been said, often by policemen, in earlier novels, raises the question of Miss Marple's basic attitude to life and to human beings. So far we have been talking about those aspects of her detection which particularly relate to her role as a little old lady in a small village. But many people, in fiction as well as in life, live in small villages and grow old in them yet do not have her prowess as a detective; apart from her gossipy sense of detail, which other people, particularly unmarried women, are shown as sharing, there are what might be called philosophical aspects of her character which give her the edge over other sleuths. These elements are her sense of humanity as weak, erring and sometimes evil, and her belief in the fixity of human character which leads her to use analogues as a major weapon in the detective process.

The notion of Miss Marple's worldliness is introduced in the first novel, *The Murder at the Vicarage*: ' "Dear Vicar," said Miss Marple, "you are so unworldly. I'm afraid that observing human nature for as long as I have done, one gets not to expect very much from it." ' This is a note that is repeated throughout the novels although sometimes it is modified into an expression of compassion for the foolishness of human nature: 'so many people seem to me not to be either bad or good, but simply, you know, very silly' (*TP*: 'TNC'). The silliness of human nature seems increasingly, as the novels progress, to include evil. By the time of *The Body in the Library*, Miss Marple is described as having a mind 'that has plumbed the depths of human iniquity' and in *The Moving Finger* (1942) as knowing 'more about the different kinds of human wickedness than anyone'. In *A Pocketful of Rye* (1953), the pessimism about human nature that Christie borrowed from her Auntie–Grannie is fully developed in Miss Marple, who 'always believes the worst. What is so sad is that one is usually justified in doing so.' By *Nemesis* (1971), the humour of an early novel like *The Murder at the Vicarage* has gone and evil rises like a miasma or like the polygonum plant which covers the grave of the too-much-loved Verity Hunt: 'Love *is* a very terrible thing. It is alive to evil, it can be one of the most evil things there can be.'

What has caused this cynicism in Miss Marple is her life in a village, and from her experience of this 'stagnant pool' she can draw conclusions which are relevant to all walks and conditions of life. Miss Marple's village parallels form the basis of her detection. At the beginning of *The Murder at the Vicarage*, she remarks that Colonel Protheroe, the murder victim, is like Joe Bucknell from the Blue Boar – both are the 'kind of man who gets the wrong idea into his head and is obstinate about it' – and this is the first of a whole crop of parallels in the novel. Dr Stone reminds her of a woman crook who pretended she 'represented the Welfare', and later of the man 'pretending to be the gas inspector' who came away with 'quite a little haul'; Lettice, Protheroe's daughter, is reminiscent of 'poor Elwell's daughter – such a pretty ethereal girl – tried to stifle her little brother'; the missing money from the church collection box recalls the money for the choir boys' outing which was taken by the organist – and so on. Some of the parallels are irrelevant or misleading, red herrings to be discarded in the final reckoning, but a correct reading of analogues, in conjunction with alertness to the minutiae of life, is what leads to the truth of the murder. Towards the end of *The Murder at the Vicarage*, Miss Marple explains to the Vicar that the study of human nature is her hobby, and since detecting a crime involves a particular focus on human nature in which motive and personality are crucial factors, it is inevitably the case that someone like Miss Marple should be successful as a detective:

> 'my hobby is – and always has been – Human Nature. So varied – and so very fascinating . . . . One begins to class people, quite definitely, just as though they were birds or flowers, group so-and-so, genus this, species that. Sometimes, of course, one makes mistakes, but less and less as time goes on. And then, too, one tests oneself . . .'
>
> (*MV*: ch. 26)

By the time of *The Body in the Library*, Miss Marple 'had attained fame by her ability to link up trivial village happenings with graver problems in such a way as to throw light upon the latter'. When Miss Marple produces one of her more eccentric parallels – 'Tommy Bond . . . and Mrs Martin, our new school-mistress. She went to wind up the clock and a frog jumped out' – one of the characters asks, 'Is the old lady a bit funny in the head?' but such dismissal of the analogous method Miss Marple uses is dangerous, as the questioner, who is discovered to be the murderer, eventually realizes.

Miss Marple's parallels are, in fact, similes and metaphors in which people are compared to other people within a fairly limited range of types. All members of the community are placed in categories whereby the unexpected, quirky, or environmentally responsive elements within human nature can be ruled out in favour of the predictability of character:

> 'I must say,' said Sir Henry ruefully, 'that I do dislike the way you reduce us all to a General Common Denominator.'
> Miss Marple shook her head sadly.
> 'Human nature is very much the same anywhere, Sir Henry.'
> '. . . I hate to intrude the personal note, but have you any parallel for *my* humble self in your village?'
> 'Well, of course, there is Briggs.'
> 'Who's Briggs?'
> 'He was the head gardener up at Old Hall. *Quite* the best man they ever had.'
>
> (*BL*: ch. 8)

The implication for a reader of a Marple novel is that differences of class and wealth (but perhaps not age and sex) count for little and that people can be read as signs by anyone with sufficient experience of the limited varieties of human nature. Although coincidence, the environment, and the unexpected may temporarily obscure the issues, in the final control Miss Marple holds over the plot and its characters, a basic metaphoric relationship is maintained in which people can be safely typed and nothing chaotic or erratic can for long prevail. This is where Miss Marple differs from Hercule Poirot whose little grey cells construct a pattern from a number of events. Miss Marple does this but she also employs what she calls 'specialized knowledge' which is a pre-existing pattern drawn from village types, a pattern into which she slots new characters. If Hercule Poirot is a rationalist, Miss Marple is a structuralist detective; having in mind a structure of human types, which she has learned from the study of her village community, all she has to do is wait for further signs to come her way. People can be assigned to categories in this deterministic view of human nature and although this by itself may not be sufficient to solve the crime, it is the necessary precondition for making sense of the circumstantial evidence that emerges. This is plainly explained in the last Marple novel Christie wrote, *Nemesis*, the most sombre and moralistic of her novels:

> 'I would not set myself up as a good judge of people,' said Miss Marple. 'I would only say that certain people remind me of certain other people that I have known, and that therefore I can presuppose a certain likeness between the way they would act.'
>
> (*N*: ch. 11)

In this novel the murderess bears a likeness not so much to a living model from St Mary Mead as to Clytemnestra from the *Agamemnon*. The human types go back through the centuries and are made permanent in great literature as much as they are in Miss Marple's memory. In *Sleeping Murder*, Gwenda screams during a performance of *The Duchess of Malfi* at the lines 'Cover her face. Mine eyes dazzle, she died young' because they recall the death of her stepmother, who, like the Duchess, was murdered by a man of 'warped and perverted mentality' who is also reminiscent of Mr Barrett of Wimpole Street, a type of man whose affection becomes 'possessive and unwholesome'.

It is her sense of character as fixed and typed that makes Miss Marple (and through her, Agatha Christie) contemptuous of modern notions that human wrongdoing may be excused because of environmental factors:

> 'If you expect me to feel sympathy, regret, urge an unhappy childhood, blame bad environment; if you expect me in fact to weep over him, this young murderer of yours, I do not feel inclined to do so. I do not like evil beings who do evil things.'
>
> (*N*: ch. 12)

In *Nemesis*, Miss Marple's confidante is Professor Wanstead who is a pathologist and a psychologist with a special interest in 'the different types of criminal brain'. His views are perhaps even more extreme than Miss Marple's:

'What I suffer in the course of my profession from people weeping and gnashing their teeth, and blaming everything on some happening in the past, you would hardly believe . . . . The misfits are to be pitied, yes, they are to be pitied if I may say so for the genes with which they are born and over which they have no control themselves.'

(*N*: ch. 12)

Character is genetically determined and this means that some people are predisposed towards murder, if the circumstances are amenable and the temptations strong enough; similarly, some people are not the type to commit murder even though in other respects they may be disreputable. Michael Raphiel in *Nemesis* is such a case: convicted of murder amidst incriminating evidence he is nevertheless 'typed' by Professor Wanstead, which includes making 'a good many physical tests', and judged to be innocent of this crime. It is even the case that encroaching senility or going 'peculiar' cannot obscure one's basic personality:

'Sometimes you just go about giving all your possessions away . . . . It shows, you see, that behind being peculiar you have quite a nice disposition. But of course if you're peculiar and behind it you have a bad disposition – well, there you are.'

(*FFFP*: ch. 25)

It is all part of the message of common sense and reassurance purveyed by classical detective fiction in which the complexities and vagaries of human personality and existence are reduced to a number of predetermined types, to a matter of genetic inheritance. If this seems arbitrary and facile – people who look you straight in the eye are often liars, women always carry handbags (and therefore if they don't they are up to no good), vicars are always unworldly, colonels bluff and maidservants adenoidal – it is in the very nature of classical detective fiction to pamper prejudice whilst appearing to pursue truth and justice.

Professor Wanstead contrasts with those psychiatrists in the Marple novels who belong, one might say, to the Laingian school of thought and who often seem incapable of distinguishing the mad from the bad. In *They Do it with Mirrors*, the psychiatrist cannot tell that Edgar Lawson is mimicking schizophrenia, and similarly in *Sleeping Murder* Dr Penrose attributes Halliday's drug-induced conviction that he has killed his wife to an 'underlying childish fixation'. Instead of doing what Miss Marple always recommends – considering the simplest explanation first, which is that the wife *had* been killed – the psychiatrist takes the mistaken Freudian path which even the patient himself rejects: 'It all sounds such poppycock. Was I in love with my mother? Did I hate my father? I don't believe a word of it . . . . I can't help feeling this is a simple police case' (ch. 10). This not only pours scorn on modern psychiatry but is also an instance of the classical detective novel defending its own territory of the logical game against the influence of Freudian theories of the irrational and unconscious. When Gwenda fears she is going mad in *Sleeping Murder* Miss Marple explains away her uncanny experiences by showing her that it was an actual memory that caused them, that they really happened. The vain and foolish Colonel Easterbrook in *A Murder is Announced* is the one who favours 'the psychological approach – that's the only thing nowadays . . . you've got to understand your criminal'. His theory is that Rudi Scherz has an inferiority complex which he tries to conceal by behaving like a cinema gangster: 'plain as a pikestaff', says the Colonel and although as a theory it may be, as a means of discovering the truth it takes no account of observation, deduction, and a knowledge of the basic types of human nature and human motivation. The Marple novels react with conservative irritation to the new psychological theories because such theories tend to deny evil and excuse the criminal and because they threaten the rationale on which detective fiction of this type depends. If people can no longer be categorized, if signs are meaningless and circumstances refuse to be made into a pattern, the danger is that the criminal will remain not only undiscovered and unpunished but also unknown and unknowable. The possibility of eliminating alien presences from society is reduced and this leaves a community vulnerable to change and decay from within.

Yet Christie's attitude towards modern psychiatric theory and practice is slightly ambivalent. She has one of her characters say, 'I'm pretty sick of the psychological jargon that's used so glibly about everything nowadays – but we can't rule it out', and in her novels and her *Autobiography* she returns frequently and vehemently to the issue of what causes wickedness and how it should be dealt with. It is a worrying and unsettled question and her interest in it becomes more complex as her novels progress. Although she says in the *Autobiography* that she has 'got more interest in my victim than in my criminals', this is hardly true; her victims in the last two Marple novels, Helen in *Sleeping Murder* and Verity in *Nemesis*, are, unlike their predecessors, innocent and likeable people but the focus of the novels is on the motives (not greed but love) of those who killed them or could have killed them. It is criminality that interests Christie, and what to do about it once it has been discovered. One of her solutions in the *Autobiography* is to transport those who are 'tainted with the germs of ruthlessness and hatred' to a 'vast land of emptiness, peopled only with primitive human beings, where man could live in simpler surroundings' (*Auto*: 454). An evolutionary theory of the development of human character seems to govern her thinking – 'the evil man nowadays may be the successful man of the past' – but it is a eugenicist's evolution: 'Perhaps Wickedness may find its physical cure . . . some day they may be able to re-arrange our genes, alter our cells.' The bleakness of this vision accords with Miss Marple's image of human life as a stagnant pool and the detective as a kind of Darwinian observer who looks at its teeming vitality through a microscope.

Some of Christie's unease at the determinism of her conceptual system is betrayed in the *Autobiography*. The discussion of evil is followed by a strange admission that being a writer, particularly a detective writer, is like being mad: 'One walks along the street . . . talking to oneself hard – not too loud I hope – and rolling one's eyes expressively and then one suddenly sees people looking at one and drawing slightly aside, clearly thinking one is mad.' The juxtaposition of an evolutionary geneticism and the rationalism and game-playing of detective fiction is indeed an anxious and contradictory one; if everything is no more than biological determinism, where then does this leave the detective, that representative figure of human autonomy, free will and logical authority? Is s/he also no more than a type, a genetically determined cypher in a semiotic system?

Christie does not, as later detective writers have done, pursue the contradiction to its deconstructive conclusions but her late Marple stories do display a claustrophobia and defeatism which contrasts with the gaiety and confidence of her early work. As Christie's sense of the existence of evil intensifies throughout the novels, so Miss Marple's character develops, or perhaps it is truer to say that the nature of her power changes and enlarges. Perhaps the solution to the problem of human weakness lies in making the detective slightly more than ordinarily human, if not God-like then certainly with some touches of divinity. 'It is miraculous', says Watson frequently of Sherlock Holmes's sleuthing prowess, and eventually, it seems, Christie also could not refrain from making Miss Marple similarly capable of extraordinary powers of detection.

Her apotheosis takes place gradually. In *The Murder at the Vicarage*, although she is described as 'that terrible Miss Marple', and although the Vicar believes that 'few things are hidden from her', her fearsome prowess is limited to psychological shrewdness and a talent for the matter-of-fact observation of events; as the Vicar says, 'There is always some perfectly good and reasonable explanation for Miss Marple's omniscience.' The earth-bound nature of her detecting continues throughout the following novels until *A Pocketful of Rye* when a new note is struck; in this novel Miss Marple is not at hand when the murders occur but makes a special journey to investigate them, actively seeking out the 'wicked murderer' because 'the wicked should not go unpunished'. As Inspector Neele recognizes, Miss Marple has assumed the role of agent of retribution: 'He was thinking to himself that Miss Marple was very unlike the popular idea of the avenging fury. And yet, he thought that was perhaps exactly what she was' (*PFR*: ch. 13). There is a suggestion in *A Pocketful of Rye* that the 'very humble and, I'm afraid, very feminine way' that Miss Marple has hitherto followed, is now being abandoned for one that is more active and vengeful, and also possessed of unearthly powers. When she arrives at Yewtree Lodge, although her pinkness and fluffiness are mentioned, so is her upright carriage and her expression of disapproval. On her hat is a bird's wing. She appears as a cross between a stern nanny or governess and a supernatural being just alighted on earth, a goddess seeking justice, or a winged Fury. What has prompted her action is, as she says on the final page, pity and anger at the killing of a vulnerable girl who was once one of her maids, and her final reaction is one of triumph because the killer will be brought to justice.

This grander dimension to Miss Marple's role is accompanied by a greater emphasis on her knitting. What begins as a harmless, spinster habit becomes a motif not merely for her gossipy, feminine kind of sleuthing but also for her role as a figure of fate, someone who knits the destiny of human beings. Mr Rafiel, in *A Caribbean Mystery*, can hardly believe that Nemesis can appear to him in 'fluffy pink wool' but he accepts the name she gives herself and in *Nemesis* itself, from beyond the grave he summons her to put right an old wrong.

> 'I envisage you sitting in a chair, a chair that is agreeable and comfortable . . . and you will spend your time mainly in knitting. I see you, as I saw you once one night as I rose from sleep disturbed by your urgency, in a cloud of pink wool . . . . If you prefer to continue knitting, that is your decision. If you prefer to serve the cause of justice, I hope that you may at least find it interesting.'
>
> (*N*: ch. 2)

What Mr Rafiel does not fully realize is that knitting and serving the cause of justice are not incompatible; in fact, the one is the insignia of the other and what began as an image of the feminine sleuth, making a pattern of the homely strands of evidence, concludes as the mark of a being who is not exactly supernatural but who represents the forces of law and justice that are the fate of those who transgress, who commit murder, which is, as Miss Marple says, a sin against God. '"[The murderer] was hanged," said Miss Marple crisply. "And a good job too. I have never regretted my part in bringing that man to justice. I've no patience with modern humanitarian scruples about capital punishment" ' (*TP*: 'A Christmas Tragedy').

Modern humanitarian scruples are represented by Dr Haydock in *The Murder at the Vicarage* whose belief that 'the day will come when we will shudder to think that we ever hanged criminals' depends on uncertainty whether there is any such thing as right or wrong:

> 'Suppose it's all a question of glandular secretion. Too much of one gland, too little of another – and you get your murderer, your thief, your habitual criminal . . . . I honestly believe crime is a case for the doctor, not the policeman and not the parson.'
> (*MV*: ch. 14)

Although the opposing view – 'Always some good reason nowadays for every dirty action that's done . . . this namby pambyism annoys me' – is given by the insensitive and opinionated Colonel Melchett, it is clear that humanitarian scruples are easily shaken when put to the test:

> We were then privileged to see exactly what Miss Marple meant by the difference between theory and practice.
> Haydock's views appeared to have undergone complete transformation. He would, I think, have liked [the murderer's] head on a charger . . .
> 'If this thing's true,' he said, 'you can count on me. The fellow's not fit to live.'
> (*MV*: ch. 31)

Lawrence Redding's willing accomplice in the murder of Colonel Protheroe and the attempted murder of Hawes, the curate, is Anne Protheroe, a woman whom the murderer intends to marry after the crime has been committed. Women are often murderers in Christie's fiction; in fact, of the Marple novels, half have women as a murderer, either alone, as in *A Murder is Announced, The Mirror Crack'd from Side to Side, At Bertram's Hotel*, and *Nemesis*, or as one of a murderous partnership, as in *The Murder at the Vicarage* and *The Body in the Library*. Statistically, this is quite unrepresentative since women commit far less murders than men. Cora Kaplan suggests that this fondness for the criminal woman is an aspect of Christie's anti-feminism; like the other Queens of Crime, she takes delight in a punitive portrayal of ambitious and sexually manipulative women as a major threat to the settled society the conservative ideology of the novels seeks to preserve. Women crime writers, Kaplan suggests, have in general been 'at worst explicitly anti-feminist and at best highly ambivalent about any disruption of traditional gender relations' (Kaplan, 1986: 18). Certainly, marriage as an institution is never attacked in Christie's novels and several of the Marple stories end with an endorsement of respectable marriage at the same time as, and in some cases as a result of, the discovery of the murderer; in *4.50 from Paddington*, Lucy Eyelesbarrow agrees to marry Bryan, in *The Body in the Library* Adelaide marries Hugo, and in *The Murder at the Vicarage* there is to be the birth of a baby to the recently married vicar and his wife. In all these cases the murders have been committed by people misusing the marriage alliance to gain wealth or class status, and these disreputable partnerships act as a foil to the virtuous marriages in the novels. A good example is the murderess in *The Body in the Library*, who herself married for reasons of financial gain through possible inheritance. She murders another whom she fears will gain the affections of the future benefactor. Finally, after the murder mystery is solved, the chastened benefactor leaves his money to the rightful inheritor, his grandson. It is as if the spurious and murderous marriage has given a necessary shock to the society it attempts to manipulate, and in doing so has reminded people of their proper duties to their families and class. In a sense, the society is better, stronger, and more assured of its traditional values, than before the murder took place.

With women who act on their own, however, the situation is no longer simply the case of a pushy woman using her sexual attractiveness to enter into a criminal partnership with a man to gain wealth and prestige. In *A Murder is Announced* it is greed which makes the murderess into a killer but greed which is understood in relation to the many years of deprivation she has suffered and the unfairness of life which has robbed her of youth and happiness. In *The Mirror Crack'd* it is a question of revenge by an actress on a woman who in the past has thought-lessly passed on a German measles infection and so caused mental abnormality in the actress's unborn child. In *At Bertram's Hotel* an amoral young woman kills because she is sexually obsessed by a man and needs wealth in order to attract and keep him. In *Nemesis* the murders have been caused by a woman's unhealthily possessive love for her adopted daughter and her jealousy of the daughter's lover. These are more in the nature of psychological murder studies, whereas the partnership novels, such as *The Murder at the Vicarage* and *The Body in the Library*, are murder stories of social alignment and property relations, with little interest in the psychology of the murderers. It is tempting to believe that the idea of the autonomous woman murderer led Christie into a greater psychological complexity, and even sympathy, when she came to write about such figures in her novels. These woman-as-murderer detective fictions rep-resent an anatomy of women's motives, characters, and tempta-tions, particularly when they are alone and must act for them-selves, which Christie also explored in her Mary Westmacott novels. *Unfinished Portrait* (1934) takes as its theme a woman desperate at her abandonment by the irresponsible man she loves; *Absent in the Spring* (1944) charts the self-exploration of a middle-aged woman marooned in the desert, particularly in regard to her possessive and autocratic behaviour towards her family; a troubled mother–daughter relationship is the theme of *A Daughter's a Daughter* (1952). The autobiographical ele-ments in these Westmacott novels found a negative projection in the figures of women murderers in Christie's detective novels. For example, the women in *At Bertram's Hotel*, *A Murder is Announced*, and *Nemesis*.

Amidst all this female criminality, Miss Marple provides the complementary component of female conscience and ration-ality. She can do this because, as an elderly spinster, she 'stands outside the sexual, familial and economic entanglements that make up the lives of most members of a community' (Kaplan, 1986: 18). Kaplan suggests that this distance from passion only serves to highlight 'the disruptive power of female sexuality in the populace at large'. But of course the removal from passion is generally true of detectives, male or female, as both Sherlock Holmes and Hercule Poirot, and even Marlowe most of the time, attest. The implication is rather that the logical processes required in detection are blunted and distorted by any emotions other than the thrill of the chase and the quest for justice. Certainly where classical detective fiction is concerned, the detective in love is not as effective as s/he might be, a fact which Dorothy L. Sayers's Harriet Vane and Peter Wimsey acknowledge. What is of interest is that Christie could only conceive of female detachment and rationality in an elderly woman; the young woman, however sensible, is eventually victim to her emotions, as Lucy Eyelesbarrow in *4.50 from Paddington* demonstrates, or she is too occupied by family ties, like Bunch Harmon in *A Murder is Announced*, or vulnerable and headstrong like Gwenda in *Sleeping Murder*. Gwenda is the young woman in the Marple books who most actively pursues a detecting role, and in this she is reminiscent of the female sleuth in Christie's Tommy and Tuppence stories. But both Gwenda and Tuppence have male partners to protect and stabilize them. If there is to be a solitary woman sleuth, it has to be an old woman.

Because she is an old woman, Miss Marple's detecting is largely sedentary and a typical Marple plot involves little travelling or activity of a physical kind. It is armchair detection in a multiple sense of the term; Miss Marple conducts the investigation from her armchair and we not only read about it from ours but also can make parallels between that investigation and our own lifestyle with its familiar terrain of sitting-room, garden, local shops, visitors to tea, and all the usual homely paraphernalia of ordinary (though middle-class) life. What Miss Marple helps us to do is not only discover the murderer in the novel but also 'read' our own world in the novel, or something sufficiently resembling it to stand in its place. The Marple novels are the folktales of twentieth-century suburban life, and Miss Marple herself is the presiding genius, the good fairy, and guide, in these narratives. The typical plot of one of her novels is, therefore, an adventure story for the middle-class, middle-aged or elderly, householding and fairly housebound British reader. *The Body in the Library* offers a classic example of such an adventure story.

It begins with a dream, Mrs Bantry's dream of a flower-show, and this suggests a certain fantasy element to the story, something of an enticing, make-believe world about to be entered, a little like the vicar's 'once upon a time' beginning to *The Murder at the Vicarage*. Nevertheless, both the contents of the dream (winning a prize for sweet peas) and Mrs Bantry's musing on her usual morning routine, suggest a secure, ordered, and prosperous world, not too removed from what the reader likes to think is reality. This world is then disrupted by a challenge (as is usually the case, one based on class and sexual threats) in the form of the strangled body of a blonde, working-class girl in the library. This is quickly followed by the marshalling of the forces of resistance, the false one (the police) and the true one (Miss Marple). It is at this point that the initiation of the detecting process takes place; several clues are laid, apparently as incidental information but actually crucial in matters of identification and taken note of only by Miss Marple: 'I was reminded', she says, on seeing the body, 'of Mrs Chetty's youngest – Edie, you know – but I think that was just because this poor girl bit her nails and her front teeth stuck out a little . . . . Edie was fond of what I call cheap finery, too' (*MV*: ch. 7). The plot then enters a stage of elaboration in which three further groups of people are introduced: the entertainers at the Majestic Hotel (Josie and Raymond), the film director Basil Blake and his wife, and the Jefferson family. Two of these groups are interlopers into the moneyed world the Bantrys represent, Basil Blake as a bohemian, the entertainers as socially mobile, would-be exploiters of the moneyed classes. The Jefferson family has one wealthy member and two hangers-on, who, like the entertainers, can be shown to be potential murderers for gain. There are also a few peripheral characters, such as the second murder victim, Pamela Reeves, and her family. The ascertaining of motives and actions now occupies this large central section of the novel during which both Miss Marple and the police assemble all the information they can. In the end, however, the first clues that Miss Marple mentions, and which the alert reader should have spotted – the bitten nails and the protruding teeth – bring the detection plot back full circle and reveal a criminal plot to divert money from its proper inheritors. The development of the story can be represented by concentric circles, the innermost one being the psychological circle which is encompassed by circles of detection, primarily Miss Marple's but also that of the police and any other characters trying to make sense of the mystery, all of which feed inwards towards the psychological heart of the plot. At the same time, there is the reverse circle of the murder plot which is being traced, as it were, backwards as the detection plot unfolds. The conduits between the various circles are those of class, money and sexuality. What happens can be represented diagrammatically, as in Figure 1.

It is the circularity, the sense of fulfilment and completion, that makes classical detective fiction so reassuring a genre to read. Its very form endorses the message it purveys of everything being all right in the end; the mysteries of fragmentary bits of information are explained, the pieces of the verbal jigsaw fit together, the reading adventure is bravely embraced and triumphantly concluded. It is, of course, particularly endearing and ingratiating that our guide through this labyrinth of verbal signs is an elderly spinster lady whose grasp of language does not always appear to be (although actually is) of the most decisive and structured; who can possibly resent such a figure of benign and oblique authority? Here she is in the denouement to *The Body in the Library* fitting the puzzle together for the benefit of the other characters and her readers. It is a denouement which is actually a tying up of loose ends, and the knot which ties the threads is, of course, marriage. This very skilfully draws attention to the inheritance ideology central to the novel (and to classical detective fiction in general) and also operates as a metaphor for the connecting up of one set of signs with another – bitten nails with cut ones, protruding teeth with receding ones – to produce, as this passage makes clear, *surety*:

Figure 1 Circular Patterns of Crime Detection in *The Body in the Library*

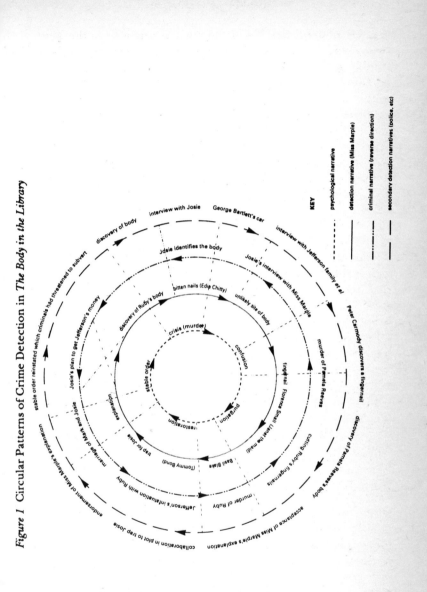

KEY

······· psychological narrative (Miss Marple)

——— detection narrative (reverse direction)

—··—·· criminal narrative (reverse direction)

— — — secondary detection narratives (police, etc)

stable order reinstated which criminals had threatened to subvert

discovery of body

interview with Josie

George Bartlett's car

interview with Jefferson family et al

Josie identifies the body

Josie's interview with Miss Marple

Peter Carmody discovers a fingernail

bitten nails (Edie Chitty)

discovery of Ruby's body

unlikely site of body

Josie's plan to get Jefferson's money

murder of Pamela Reeves

crisis (murder)

confusion

fingernail Florence Small (Jane the maid)

discovery of Pamela Reeves' body

stable order

purgation

murder of Ruby

unpleasure

restoration

Cutting Ruby's fingernails

acceptance of Miss Marple's explanation

marriage of Mark and Josie

trap for Josie (Tommy Bond)

Basil Blake

Jefferson's infatuation with Ruby

endorsement of Miss Marple's explanation

collaboration in plot to trap Josie

'I now had two *halves* of the case, and both quite convincing, but they did not fit. There must *be* a connection, but I could not find it . . . . If it had not been for Dinah Lee I shouldn't have thought of it – the most obvious thing in the world. Somerset House! Marriage! . . . If either of those two was married . . . .

'But, of course, really, in my own mind, I *knew*. You couldn't get away, could you, from those bitten nails . . . . *Bitten* nails and close *cut* nails are quite different! Nobody could mistake them who knew anything about girls' nails – . . . .

'People *will* talk too much. Mark Gaskell talked too much. He was speaking of Ruby and he said "her teeth ran down her throat." But the dead girl in Colonel Bantry's library had teeth that stuck *out* . . . .

'It's so nice to be *sure*, isn't it?'

'Sure is the word,' said Conway Jefferson grimly.

(*BL*: ch. 18)

Chapter Four

MISS MARPLE'S AFTERLIFE

OWADAYS EVERYONE knows Miss Marple. Even people who have never read an Agatha Christie detective novel are aware of the character, perhaps more than they are of Hercule Poirot, Lord Peter Wimsey, or Chandler's Marlowe. In the world of fictional detection, it is really only Sherlock Holmes who is more famous, and who has more thoroughly entered the language as the name not just of a literary character but of an activity, a way of thinking and behaving. Certainly, as Michael Davie pointed out in the *Observer* of 27 December 1987, Miss Marple is the best known of all women sleuths, not least because of her posthumous existence on stage and screen – on the Christmas Day preceding his article half the nation had watched *4.50 from Paddington* on TV. On Christmas Day 1989, a similar audience watched *A Caribbean Mystery* on BBC1, directed by Chris Petit and featuring the 84-year-old Joan Hickson as Miss Marple, the actress considered by the Christie family to be nearest to the author's conception of the character and now seemingly established by general consent as the definitive Miss Marple. *A Caribbean Mystery* is the last of a series which has brought fame to Christie's elderly spinster detective and endeared her to millions.

Before Joan Hickson, Miss Marple had a somewhat chequered career on stage, film, and television, and she seems to have had to wait for BBC-TV's particular skills in casting and in the creation of period atmosphere to find herself satisfyingly transformed from written word to visual image. As far as the stage is concerned, her most successful appearance seems to have been in a dramatization by Christie herself of *The Murder at the Vicarage* produced by Moie Charles and Barbara Toy which had its London opening in December 1949 at the Playhouse Theatre and played for four months. Barbara Mullen created the Miss Marple role and the play was directed by Reginald Tate who also played Laurence Redding. According to Charles Osborne (Osborne, 1982: 55), the play was transposed to a post-war, contemporary setting which must have lent an air of modernity to its particular brand of conservative escapism. The play was regularly acted by amateur and repertory companies and was revived on the London stage at the Savoy Theatre in 1975, with Barbara Mullen again playing the part of Miss Marple. This time, the play ran for two years, a reasonable success, although small by comparison with *The Mousetrap. A Murder is Announced* also found its way to the stage in 1975 but this was less successful, perhaps because it has an intricate plot which contains many characters who could be confusingly similar on stage. Its slightly unlikely ending, where Miss Marple mimics the voice of a dead woman from a cupboard, appeared merely facetious, according to Osborne, who also thought the characterization of Miss Marple resulted in an unfortunate mix of Hilda Doolittle and a troublesome granny, rather than the all-perceiving, shrewd lady detective of the novels.

This kind of problem in portraying Miss Marple on stage, and also on screen, seems to have been recurrent and perhaps stems from the difficulty of portraying old age in comedy. To a certain extent, Christie has contributed to the stereotype of geriatric foolishness and risibility in her presentation of a dithering old lady whose hesitations and self-interruptions are intended to mask a cool, detached intellect. Margaret Rutherford, who was the first embodiment of Miss Marple on the cinema screen, and who played her in the four MGM films of the early 1960s, emphasized the dotty element in the character but in no way captured the quietness and sharpness that the novels suggest. Rutherford was also far more domineering and bossy than the Miss Marple of the novels, a characteristic particularly evident in the first of the MGM films, *Murder, She Said* (1961), which was based on *4.50 from Paddington*. Under the direction of George Pollock, Margaret Rutherford played Miss Marple as an energetic, eccentric, and slightly confused 60-year-old brigadier-spinster who, unlike her frail counterpart in the novel, needs no Lucy Eyelesbarrow to do her sleuthing for her and gets a job as a maid at the Crackenthorpe home where she dominates the action in a way that the novel's Miss Marple does not. *The Times* commented that it was an unambitious film which yet had 'the immense advantage of a plot written by an expert. Not vintage Christie, perhaps, but as ingenious as ever, with clues and red herrings abounding'. In fact, Christie had not written the script and thought it 'pretty poor': '*I* could have made it more exciting' (Morgan, 1984: 328). Yet she dedicated her next novel, *The Mirror Crack'd from Side to Side*, to Margaret Rutherford who had at least given an enjoyable performance in *Murder, She Said*, even though 'not much like Miss Marple' (Morgan, 1984: 335). The next MGM Marple film, *Murder at the Gallop*, however, Christie thought 'incredibly silly'; based on a Poirot novel, *After the Funeral*, it has Miss Marple, who replaces Poirot, joining a riding academy in order to investigate the death of an elderly recluse. This is a style of comedy appropriate to the broad and exaggerated acting manner of Margaret Rutherford but it in no way faithfully reproduced the character in the novels. *The Times* thought that 'the whole thing is happily calculated to convince foreigners yet again that everything they have been told about the English is absolutely true and only a trifle understated'.

The same recipe of Pollock-Rutherford, Marple for Poirot, was repeated in a third film, *Murder Most Foul* ('Can you imagine a triter title?', Christie said), loosely based on *Mrs McGinty's Dead*, but in the next Marple film, *Murder Ahoy!* (1964), an entirely original script was provided by David Pursall and Jack Seddon in which Miss Marple is most improbably found on a Royal Navy training ship. Christie was appalled: 'to have one's characters incorporated in somebody else's film seems to me monstrous and highly unethical' (Morgan, 1984: 335). *The Times* critic remarked that 'Marples [*sic*] fans will have reservations, but Rutherford fans will have none.' The drift towards farce, and the eclipsing of a character in a novel by the personality of the actress who played her, came to a halt in 1964 when the contract with MGM was terminated, Christie being finally outraged by the proposal to change Poirot into 'some sort of gorilla or private eye – and a lot of violence and brutality' (Morgan, 1984: 337). In a much-quoted interview with Francis Wyndham in 1966, she expressed her unequivocal dislike of what had happened to her novels in the hands of MGM:

> I kept off films for years because I thought they'd give me too many heartaches. Then I sold the rights to MGM, hoping they'd use them for television. But they chose films. It was too awful! They did things like taking a Poirot and putting Miss Marple in it! And all the climaxes were so poor, you could see them coming! I get an unregenerate pleasure when I think they're not being a success. They wrote their own script for the last one – nothing to do with me at all – *Murder Ahoy!* One of the silliest things you ever saw! It got very bad reviews, I'm delighted to say.
> (Quoted in Osborne, 1982: 203)

There were to be two more attempts at a full feature Miss Marple film before she was to become a BBC television series. A team which had produced *Death on the Nile* and *Murder on the Orient Express*, attempted a similar box office success with *The Mirror Crack'd from Side to Side* (1980), directed by Guy Hamilton. The success of the earlier films had rested partly on gripping plots but more on the use of well-known stars such as Peter Ustinov, Bette Davis, Jacqueline Bisset, and Lauren Bacall, often for minor roles, and the luxurious and nostalgic settings of a pre-war Nile steamer and an international train. The same was attempted in *The Mirror Crack'd*; aptly, the wealthy, neurotic actress in her fifth marriage is played by Elizabeth Taylor, with Rock Hudson as her current husband. Geraldine Chaplin, Kim Novak, and Tony Curtis have minor roles, and Edward Fox is the police inspector. Angela Lansbury is Miss Marple, perhaps rather young and round (Miss Marple is described in the novels as tall and thin) but not unacceptable except that she is hampered by a badly written script and the rather slow and tableau-esque movement of the plot.

The final Marple film, *A Caribbean Mystery*, was made for television with Helen Hayes as an even more cuddly Miss

Marple, and hints of romantic interest are called up both with the murder victim, Major Palgrave, who no longer has a glass eye, and with Mr Rafiel, never a dying man as he is in the novel but transformed into a sprightly, bouquet-swinging admirer. The film is at its most un-Christie-ish when Miss Marple dons a pirate's costume for a fancy dress party.

After these variously grotesque and farcical presentations, BBC television's series of Marple dramatizations appeared as refreshingly true to the novels and also tastefully evocative of the small-village and comfortable middle-class life which are the novels' usual setting. Along with the recent screening of three of Dorothy L. Sayers's Peter Wimsey novels, Marjorie Allingham's Albert Campion novels, and, on ITV, some of Christie's Poirot stories, the Marple TV series is in the current mood of nostalgia for the interbellum and post-war years, and also testifies to the continuing popularity of classical detective novels.

The tone of the BBC Marple series is established by the plaintively cheerful introductory music and by the sketch-book illustrations which accompany the opening credits. Joan Hickson's Miss Marple is an earnest, tweed-clad, soft-spoken gentlewoman who sometimes seems a little flustered and illogical, in a genteel way, but nevertheless convinces the viewer of her intelligence and moral strength. Joan Hickson's particular contribution to the evolution of the character is her head-on-one-side, shrewd and evaluative gaze, which perhaps gives a more penetrating and disconcerting impression than the novels of how Miss Marple looks. There have been ten adaptations so far and all have closely followed Christie's dialogue, generally reckoned to be one of her strongest points. What changes there have been to the plots have been concerned to keep the main line of detective enquiry clearly before the viewer, so that in *The Murder at the Vicarage*, for instance, the sub-plots concerning Dr Stone and Griselda's affair with Redding have been pruned. In exchange, the village setting is given in loving detail, with shots of the church, of Mrs Lestrange's house, and of Miss Marple in her garden in cosy proximity to the vicarage garden with its artist's atelier. The comic and mistaken hostility of Inspector Slack towards Miss Marple is repeated in this play from *The Body in the Library* (the first to be televised) and given a variant in Inspector Craddock's suspicion and eventual capitulation in the later *A Murder is Announced*. In *At Bertram's Hotel* the slow start to the televised version allows for the full impact of nostalgia in the opening scenes as the viewer savours the majestic organization, perfect service and Edwardian food ('old-fashioned beef-steak pudding . . . great sirloins of beef and saddles of mutton, and an old-fashioned English tea and a wonderful English breakfast') of this fraudulent hotel. Equally successful, largely due to excellent casting, is *A Murder is Announced*, adapted by Alan Plater and directed by David Giles.

In some respects the BBC television versions are even more effective than the novels. Whilst keeping to the basic plots of the novels and retaining the *frissons* of the classic detective story – the threat to property, the hygienic violence of the murder, the unknown criminal in our midst, the disturbance of the established order – the dramas are presented with a visual attention to period detail which the novels do not pretend to. This gives them a further dimension of nostalgia and assurance. To the traditional pleasures of the detective plot are added the visual delights of the cars and clothes of a previous age, the houses without television aerials (a nice touch, that), the types of people we believe were around then, most particularly the type of the old lady, everyone's favourite aunt or grandmother. If the novels offer a fantasy of order restored through the processes of logic and categorization, this is a fantasy which is intensified in the 'realism' of their television dramatization. Television, particularly the high-quality productions which have made the Marple series so popular, substantiates the unreal world of detective fiction. St Mary Mead begins to look like a real village and not the stereotypical setting that Christie used as all that was necessary to get her plots going. The village may be a sentimental figment of our imagination but TV visually recreates it for us in the comfort of our own homes, temporarily destroys it through the actions of the criminal, and then reconstitutes it in all its imagined harmonies before our very eyes, unmediated by even the arduous and distancing act of reading. The notion of the armchair detective is given yet a further dimension.

If Miss Marple continues to survive in the visual adaptation that TV provides, she also has an indirect afterlife in the development of the woman detective in post-war fiction, particularly from the 1970s onwards. As we pointed out in Chapter One, during the years after the First World War, women made of detective fiction a genre that suited them. Though none of the well-known women detective writers of this time – Christie, Sayers, Marsh, Allingham – were declared feminists, they nevertheless partook of attitudes created by feminism, as well as by the changed conditions for women brought about by the war. In detective fiction they found a genre which flourished in domestic and circumscribed settings: a family, a village, or a similar kind of closed community (such as the women's college in Dorothy L. Sayers' *Gaudy Night*). Within the apparent realism and respectability of these 'female' worlds, Christie and her kind could exercise a fascination with violence and evil and, more importantly, with the power of rationality to control events and the destinies of other people. For them, the detective novel was an enabling genre: rational, humorous, freed from the contamination of romance, an intellectual enterprise to be entered into on equal terms with men.

Since then, a second wave of feminism has occurred and in its aftermath women seem again to be finding in detective fiction a means of exploring ideas about power and morality. According to Alison Hennegan (in Green, 1989), the appeal of detective fiction in this respect is hardly surprising since it is a genre 'deeply concerned with the making and breaking of social codes, the apportionment of guilt and blame and the processes of judgment and punishment' (Hennegan, 1989: 3). In her opinion, women have rarely had a fair deal from legal processes – 'all too often there has been one law for men and another for women' – and therefore natural justice, which takes account of sin as well as criminality, seems particularly attractive. Detective fiction, which is unfettered by the constraints of the legal system, can explore the issues which lie outside the law, or in opposition to it, or which are judged immaterial in a court of law. Hennegan says that at 'any point where specifically female needs and experience run counter to man-made laws and systems, you will find a woman crime novelist examining that conflict'.

Christie would not have subscribed to the feminism of that statement but it is the case that her novels, however intellectualized and conservative their detecting processes may seem, do often take a woman's view of the crime, or of the social issues that surround the crime. Christie's Miss Marple stories are concerned with natural justice, and it is for this reason that we are adding a further 'afterthought' on Miss Marple which links her to those women detectives who belong to the novels of this latest phase of the feminist movement. These are her daughters, granddaughters and great-granddaughters, and in them she has another kind of afterlife.

As far as English women detective writers are concerned, the obvious modern successors to Christie are Ruth Rendell and P.D. James, not least in popularity and commercial success. Both these writers enlarge the scope of the detective novel in the psychological complexity of their characterization and the social realism which provides the context of the crime. The game element is less pronounced than in Christie, and their novels are bulky and 'serious' in ways that hers never pretended to be. For instance, P.D. James's recent novel, *Devices and Desires* (1989), is 407 pages long and its plot is centred on a nuclear power station. Who did the murder(s) in this story is of less importance than the debate on nuclear power and various social issues, in particular the relationship between parents and children, one of James's recurrent concerns.

Adam Dalgliesh is the detective in this latest James novel and he is obviously her chief and favoured detective. Unlike Rendell, however, James has given space to women detectives and one of these, Cordelia Gray, who first appeared in the appropriately named *An Unsuitable Job for a Woman* (1972), can be described as one of the first of the new 'feminist' detectives of the modern period as far as English writing is concerned.

Like Shakespeare's heroine, Cordelia is the motherless daughter of an egocentric father, a wandering anarchist who gave her an unusual, disorganized childhood. She also has two detective fathers: the failed policeman Bernie, who taught her the rudiments of detecting and bequeathed a detective agency to her, and, of course, Commander Adam Dalgliesh. Intuitive, intellectual, distant, slightly effete, Dalgliesh is Cordelia's standard of what a good detective should be, even though her own methods are more impulsive and emotional, and also more prone to violence, than his.

Much more than Miss Marple, Cordelia Gray is a vulnerable, fallible detective, continuing the process begun by Christie of cutting the detective down to size, bringing him/her within the range of the ordinary. Cordelia has less control over events than Miss Marple, and the clues are less accessible to her reasoning. She is thrown down a well in *An Unsuitable Job for a Woman* and down a sea cave in *The Skull beneath the Skin* (1982) and both these novels conclude as much with her defeat as her success. Where she does succeed, it is with nowhere near the omniscience of Miss Marple. She is also less law-abiding; unlike her very respectable predecessor, she does not always collaborate with the police but carries with her a residue of her anarchic upbringing and the beginning of an attitude of suspicion towards the police which many later feminist detective writers have projected. This is related to her ambivalent attitudes towards the crime and the criminal, indeed, towards (male) authority in general. In *An Unsuitable Job for a Woman*, for instance, she hides the identity of the murderer from even Dalgliesh because she lets her sympathy for a female murderer overrule her professional ethics.

With *A Taste for Death* (1986), P.D. James introduced a female police detective as an assistant to Dalgliesh, no doubt in response to the increase in the numbers of women police officers and their growing professionalism. Kate Miskin has been chosen by Dalgliesh because she possesses the qualities he most admires in a detective: 'intelligence, courage, discretion and common sense'. He also thinks her presence may help to dilute the 'collusive and macho freemasonry which frequently bound together a team of all male officers'. Kate Miskin herself is under the very female pressure of trying to reconcile the demands of a professional life to which she is passionately dedicated with domestic responsibilities, in this case the care of an ailing and demanding grandmother. As a result of Kate's police activities, her grandmother is violently attacked and dies at the end of the novel, which perhaps suggests that the double demands on a woman detective of work and home are incompatible, or at least difficult to reconcile. Nevertheless, Kate survives, Dalgliesh is sympathetic, and in this development the woman detective becomes even more a figure with whom the female reader can identify.

In some respects this is not the case with Antonia Fraser's Jemima Shore (*Quiet as a Nun*, 1977, and *The Wild Island*, 1978) who is a highly romanticized detective, a left-wing investigative reporter who nevertheless has a luxurious, stylish lifestyle and whose sexual behaviour is unprofessional – for instance, on one occasion she sleeps with one of the suspects. She is a kind of female James Bond and the plots she is part of are as unlikely and melodramatic as his. Yet in spite of her extravagant behaviour, Jemima is by no means the omniscient detective; far less than Miss Marple (and James Bond) is she in control of events and the truth takes her by surprise rather than being uncovered by her through logical processes. In this respect she is ordinary and this continues the drift towards the human and fallible that is a feature of recent detective writing. As Craig and Cadogan say, the events and characters described in both Fraser's novels are 'quite preposterous' but this increase in fantasy is matched by an increase in the realism of the detection process: Jemima Shore is not 'the powerful outsider who has got everything under control [and] is as startled as anyone when the truth comes out' (Craig and Cadogan, 1986: 237).

Neither James nor Fraser would describe themselves as feminist writers and although they depict lively, independent detecting heroines, these young women, however unorthodox their sleuthing methods, do not see their work as constituting a critique of patriarchal society. For the beginnings of that one has to turn to the United States to see in the novels of Amanda

Cross the introduction of the 'new feminist' woman detective who ambivalently occupies the basically conservative genre of detective fiction to explore the morality and politics of progressive feminism and as a form of resistance to the pressures of heterosexual capitalism. Amanda Cross, pseudonym for the feminist literary critic Carolyn Heilbrun, first appeared as this kind of detective writer in 1964 with *In the Last Analysis*. This, and later novels – *The James Joyce Murder* (1967), *Poetic Justice* (1970), *The Theban Mysteries* (1971), *A Death in the Faculty* (1981) and *A Trap for Fools* (1989), for example – follow Sayers's example in *Gaudy Night* in exposing the murderous opposition to feminism, and to women in general, which abounds in an academic community. Heilbrun's debt to Sayers is openly acknowledged in *Writing a Woman's Life* where she admits that Sayers's novel helped her through an uncertain period of her life: 'I was recreating myself', Heilbrun wrote; 'Women come to writing . . . simultaneously with self-creation . . . . Sayers provided a fantasy, of course – all detective novels are fantasies – but at least hers was not the romantic fantasy long prescribed for women' (Heilbrun, 1989: 52).

Heilbrun's detective, Kate Fansler, is as much a wish-fulfilment fantasy for Heilbrun as Harriet Vane was for Sayers:

> Without children, unmarried, unconstrained by the opinion of others, rich and beautiful, the newly created Kate Fansler now appears to me a figure out of never-never land. That she seems less a fantasy figure these days – when she is mainly criticised for drinking and smoking too much, and for having married – says more about the changing mores, and my talents as prophet, than about my intentions at the time. I wanted to give her everything and see what she could do with it. Of course, she set out on a quest (the male plot), she became a knight (the male role), she rescued a (male) princess.
>
> (Heilbrun, 1989: 115)

Like Heilbrun, Kate Fansler combines a career as a Professor of Literature with a semi-official job as a sleuth. In this she initiates (or perhaps continues, if one allows Harriet Vane in *Gaudy Night* to be included) a line of detective novels in which a woman lecturer in English Literature is the sleuth; it seems to be a parallel activity to the critical reading of texts, or perhaps a metaphor for it. There is also opportunity for a light-hearted display of learning, even of virtuosity. Amanda Cross's novels are heavily literary and part of their appeal lies in the cross-referencing to famous texts and authors. They are also written in a quasi-academic style – 'full of subordinate clauses, and penultimate climaxes, interspersed with periodic sentences', as Fansler herself says – and this tends to limit their readership to those who can share the joke. In *The James Joyce Murder*, for instance, each chapter is called after a story from Joyce's *Dubliners* and the plot revolves around a lost story by him which has been concealed in a bale of hay. Kate Fansler not only has to help solve this crime but also ponder whether to become president of Jay College for Women and whether to marry Reed Amhearst: a full life, very different from Miss Marple, and the novels have a kind of racy knowingness which makes them, for all their right-on attitudes, more elitist than Christie's. They do, however, have an overt feminist thrust, or at least a woman-centred thrust, which typically involves the discovery of a female tradition, often one to do with writing, so that Kate Fansler's sleuthing almost literarily echoes Virginia Woolf's belief that if we want to create ourselves, as women and as writers, we must 'think back through our mothers'. In Cross's seventh novel, *Sweet Death, Kind Death* (1984), for example, Kate is found attempting to help in the organization of a Women's Studies programme in a conservative college whilst at the same time investigating the death of a well-known, eccentric feminist academic whose 'suicide' note refers to the death of the nineteenth-century writer Charlotte Perkins Gilman. It is a far cry from St Mary Mead, and Miss Marple's attempts to salvage the past. Kate also lacks Miss Marple's sureties concerning good and evil yet each would recognize in the other those qualities of intellectual coolness and moral alertness which make them sisters under the skin.

In Valerie Miner's *Murder in the English Department* (1982) the enclosed village community of classic detective fiction is once again exchanged for the enclosed community of academia. Nan Weaver, untenured, working class, and feminist, finds her posi-

tion in the English Department made difficult by the conservative, misogynist Angus Murchie. Nan's problems are exacer-
bated by her inevitable involvement in a campaign against
sexual harassment, all of which reaches a climax when Angus
Murchie is found stabbed on New Year's Eve, apparently by a
woman he was trying to rape. The plot in this novel is fairly
straightforward with none of Christie's narrative ingenuity but
this is obviously of less importance in Valerie Miner than the
issues her murder story explores and the processes of self-
discovery the three main women characters undergo during it.

Both Cross and Miner are North American writers; a British
version of the academic detective story is provided by Joan
Smith's enjoyable and well-crafted *A Masculine Ending* (1988)
and *Why Aren't They Screaming* (also 1988). The detective,
Loretta Lawson, is a lecturer in English Literature at one of the
London colleges but the literary allusions are more subtly and
sparingly used in these novels. The title of *Why Aren't They
Screaming*, for instance, is taken from a poem by Philip Larkin,
'The Old Fools'; ironically, the fools in Smith's novel are not the
old people close to death of Larkin's poem but the old guard,
the establishment, mainly the police, who cannot believe that a
Tory MP could be guilty of murder and who also cannot
sympathize with those who wish to prevent nuclear war. The
novel is set against the background of the American bombing of
Libya, the women's peace camps outside the US bases, USAF
intimidation, and the resignation of Cecil Parkinson. Loretta,
convalescent after glandular fever, stays to investigate the
murder of her landlady out of loyalty to a working-class girl from
the peace camp; but the girl is killed, no one, not even her
journalist husband, believes Loretta's version of events, and the
novel ends with the Tory MP promoted to a ministerial position
at the Ministry of Defence. Loretta's lack of success in flushing
out the criminal marks a major difference between this and a
Miss Marple novel, but in other respects there are similarities;
although Loretta is an academic, the novel's action takes place
in a village, and its tight plotting, skilful use of red herrings, and
the credibility and rationality of its detection processes are
reminiscent of classical detective fiction.

With Barbara Wilson the attempt to transform an essentially conservative, rationalist, law-abiding, and male-oriented genre into a vehicle for radical feminist views receives a further twist. *Murder in the Collective* (1984) exposes the contradictions of the liberal, anti-racist, anti-sexist individual who nevertheless enjoys the authority of playing detective and discovering the truth. In a murder story in which two radical printing collectives attempt to merge, the self-appointed sleuth, Pam Nilsen, finds that she not only exposes the dishonesties of her colleagues but also the arrogance and ruthlessness of the detective role itself. Her assumption that she can, as a white, liberal, 'objective' woman, completely understand and judge the situation is deflated when, in the final chapters, she is forced to empathize with the murderer whom she does not reveal to the police. Inherent in Miss Marple's success as a detective was a sense of the single-mindedness of her pursuit of justice, which made her into a figure of Nemesis. For all her initial desire similarly to hunt out the truth, Pam Nilsen has none of Miss Marple's assurance of the rightness of her cause. In a later novel, *Sisters of the Road* (1987), this indecision and vulnerability is even more painfully explored when Pam, hunting the killer of several prostitutes on the seedy side of her native Seattle, is raped by the killer and forced into a difficult process of self-evaluation during her convalescence. In *The Dog Collar Murders* (1989), Pam's lesbianism is put under test when she has to face the possibility that lesbians may be as violent and lustful as 'straight' members of society. In these novels the detective is also a victim, or potential victim, a theme explored in a British novel, Rebecca O'Rourke's *Jumping the Cracks* (1987), in which the heroine's energies are more absorbed in keeping herself both solvent and free from harm than in solving a murder she accidentally stumbles upon. In a short story by O'Rourke, 'Standing Witness' (*Reader, I Murdered Him*, ed. Green, 1989), the 'detective' does no more than stand at her window in the small hours and reconstruct in imagination what has led to the scene of police activity round a body in a car in the street below.

Very different is Helen Keremos, the lesbian detective of Eve Zaremba's novels. Helen is a professional: 'Helen Keremos. I detect', she announces in *Beyond Hope* (1987) and she is tough and active, Marlowe-like in her dead-pan decisiveness and her prose-style:

> A decision had to be made, fast. Putting an arm around her shoulders I lifted her to a sitting position . . . . I pulled her feet off the bed hoping she could stand up. No way. Her body was as flaccid as a string puppet. She had to be carried. I put my left shoulder to her middle and with a groan got her up in a fire-fighter's carry. She felt like the newly dead, totally relaxed, her head hitting the small of my back.
>
> (*Beyond Hope.* 84)

Needless to say, Helen's activities are not confined to village life but are wildly international and her sleuthing brings breath-taking exposure to terrorism, arms smuggling, and spying as well as murder. Miss Marple would no doubt say that life in the mountains of the Canadian–US border is much like that in St Mary Mead and the megalomaniac Huber quite similar to the local doctor but even she could not claim that Helen's hit-and-grab detecting methods bear much resemblance to those practised in classical detective fiction.

Even more hard-boiled and Marlowe-ish are the novels of Mary Wings, *She Came Too Late* (1986) and *She Came in a Flash* (1988). The appropriately named lesbian hero, Emma Victor, talks and thinks out of the side of her mouth – 'I could feel a tender egg growing above my cheek. Someone had tried to remodel my face, and they hadn't stuck around to see the results' – frequently gets busted up and, of course, fails to save the object of her search. In *She Came in Flash* this is Lana Flax, a once brilliant young physicist who has now become a victim of the Vishnu Divine Inspiration Commune and is found drowned with her feet embedded in concrete. Wings's books are vivid, violent, and sexy and may perhaps rather be described as feminist thrillers than detective stories; certainly their detection plots are subordinate to other concerns – love affairs, food, California, meditation, disco dancing, self-discovery.

Equally though differently remote from the Christie mode is Dorothy Bryant's witty and sophisticated *Killing Wonder* (1982),

where the interest is as much in the relationship between women and writing as it is in solving the murder mystery. Bryant's
detective, Jessamyn Posey, is of Italian-Chinese parentage and
her detecting, contrary to the pattern of classic detection, is
done through psychic powers. So different is a story like this
from Christie's model that it strains the definition to classify
both types as detective novels. Yet they do have basic features in
common, primarily a detective who, however imperfectly and
self-doubtingly, takes it upon herself to discover the truth of the
crime. In Christie, the crime is simply murder; in modern
feminist detective stories the murder is merely a symptom of
other crimes and other puzzles which have to be solved, puzzles
to do with being a woman in late capitalist society.

The popularity of the new woman's detective story for both
writers and readers is indicated, and also encouraged, by the
entry of the major feminist publishing houses into crime
publishing. Virago and the Women's Press now have their crime
lists of new writers and Pandora has started a Women's Crime
Writers series (Pandora Whodunnits) which aims, its editors
say, 'to reprint the best of women crime writers who have
disappeared from print and to introduce a new generation of
women crime writers to all devotees of the genre. We also hope
to seduce new readers to the pleasures of detective fiction.' Not
many of the novels reprinted from earlier periods have women
detectives but they nevertheless confirm a tradition of women
writers within this genre and restore to us delights such as
Christianna Brand's *Green for Danger* (1945) and *London
Particular* (1952). In her introduction to *London Particular* P.D.
James claims a kind of descent from it in praising its 'credible
characters . . . strong sense of place [and] a cleverly clued
detective story': thinking back through our mothers indeed.

This recent upsurge of feminist crime publishing has also
seen the publication of a number of anthologies, reminiscent,
of course, of Dorothy L. Sayers's *Omnibus of Crime* (1928) and
equally indicative of a current popularity. A British example is
the wittily titled *Reader, I Murdered Him* (Green, 1989), an anthology of original crime stories edited by Jan Green. In a similar
American anthology, *The Womansleuth Anthology: Contemporary*

Mystery Stories by Women (1988), the editor, Irene Zahava, maintains that this new detective fiction realistically reflects the lives of contemporary women, and places women detectives in the forefront of the genre. 'Characters such as Cordelia Gray, Kate Fansler, Anna Lee, Norah Mulchaney, V.I. Warshawksi, Kinsey Millhone, and many others, have broken away from the macho mould' of much previous detective writing and their authors have introduced topics and settings, such as unemployment, domestic violence and inner city poverty, which are the substance of many women's lives. A realist tendency always present in classic detective fiction is now fully developed in the downbeat lifestyle of the modern female detective and the vulnerable ordinariness of her sleuthing activities.

In fact, it is not just 'realism' which features in these stories but a political radicalism which is often at odds with the traditional assumptions of the detective story. In 'The Permanent Personal Secretary' by Jane Burke (in *Reader, I Murdered Him*), for instance, solidarity between women is more important than telling the police the truth, and this is also true of 'Teddy' by Sue Ward. The practice of a kind of natural justice according to the beliefs of the detectives themselves is even more prominent in Gillian Slovo's novels, *Morbid Symptoms* (1984), *Death by Analysis* (1986) and *Death Comes Staccato* (1987), where the narrator runs a detective agency together with a black woman assistant, Carmen. Progressive detectives indeed, they research the policies with regard to racism and sexism of firms wishing to do contract work for the GLC and for the separate London boroughs. An anti-racist, anti-sexist, anti-homophobic position is important in these novels, as also in Barbara Wilson's fiction, and overrules the genre's traditional demands for legal retribution. This constitutes a development which would have completely undercut the ideological basis of the classic detective novel.

As we have seen, lesbian detectives are an important feature of much new detective fiction. If, during the inter-war years, the spinster was the odd woman whose marginalized relationship to orthodox society made her into an effective detective, her role has now been overtaken by that of the lesbian sleuth whose alienated approach to the crimes of patriarchy enables her to see truths that others cannot see. One of the most amusing and inventive examples of this kind of new lesbian detective fiction is 'The Adventure of the Perpetual Husbands' by Ellen Dearmore (in *The Womansleuth Anthology*) in which Gertrude Stein and Alice B. Toklas investigate the infamous and historical Landru case. Departing from Stein's well-documented love of detective stories, Dearmore builds a plot based on Alice's attempt to sell a typewriter, which could have brought her into contact with Landru. Both women set out to solve the crime, weaving their way through motifs filched from Stein's autobiographies – Alice sitting with the wives of the famous, Gertrude's love of boxing, her sitting 'knee to knee' with Hemingway, Alice's jealousy over this, and so on, even to the pastiche of Stein's style:

> His Christian name, Henri, which turned out not to be so Christian after all. But *Henri*. Doesn't that bring to mind Henry VIII, who had six wives and murdered two of them? To this unfortunate name of Henri was added the even more difficult name Désiré. To desire. That explains the 283 lovers. You know my theory about names: to name is to claim, to name is to blame, to name is to determine. In this case it obviously determined.

In a lesbian revision of the Holmes and Watson relationship, Stein and Toklas set about the mystery in different but equally orthodox ways, Stein 'thinking thoughts' which lead her to general conclusions concerning the evils of American capitalism, while Toklas, the intuitive one, is busy checking Landru's astrological chart: 'Tauruses love to dig in the earth.' Arriving early at Landru's villa, Alice notices lorries driving to garbage pits and concludes they are the burial grounds of the victims. The story ends with Gertrude claiming the credit for the discovery, but Alice has the last word, rejoicing that there is now one less subject for Gertrude and Hemingway to talk about. The story neatly mixes fact and fiction (as did Stein's autobiographies), it gives a lesbian twist to the detective couple immortalized in Holmes and Watson, and it validates two kinds of detective methods, the rational and the intuitive. Stein, as the thinking armchair detective in the manner of Holmes and of Marple, arrives at a general conception of the misogyny inherent in most crime, whilst Toklas actually divines the 'facts' of this particular crime by means of the irrational processes of astrology.

Stein and Toklas were contemporaries of Christie and it is interesting to see the ghosts of these inter-war women evoked in the newest phase of women's detective writing. Perhaps the next twist in the spiral will be a resurrection of Miss Marple herself, or if not exactly Miss Marple, then an elderly detective spinster rather like her who will take on the crimes of the last two decades of the twentieth century. The ageing population that we are told is shortly going to be a burden on the British economy would surely relish such a figure who could wreak fictional vengeance on an uncharitable and patronizing society. In the mean time, the woman's detective novel is very much alive and kicking in its new feminist colours, demonstrating that it is as much an empowering genre for today's women writers exploring questions of justice and morality as it was for Christie when she caused Miss Marple to fathom the puzzle of human behaviour in the microcosmic backwater of St Mary Mead.

APPENDIX:
LIST OF NOVELS MENTIONED
IN CHAPTER FOUR

Brand, Christianna (1945) *Green for Danger*, London: Pandora Press [1987].
—— (1952) *London Particular*, London: Pandora Press [1988].
Bryant, Dorothy (1982) *Killing Wonder*, London: The Women's Press, first published in New York: Ata Books, 1981.
Cross, Amanda (1967) *The James Joyce Murder*, London: Virago [1989].
—— (1970) *Poetic Justice*, New York: Avon [1979].
—— (1971) *The Theban Mysteries*, New York: Avon [1979].
—— (1981) *A Death in the Faculty*, London: Virago [1988].
—— (1984) *Sweet Death, Kind Death*, London: Virago [1988].
—— (1989) *A Trap for Fools*, London: Virago [1990].
Fraser, Antonia (1977) *Quiet as a Nun*, London: Viking Penguin.
—— (1978) *The Wild Island*, London: Weidenfeld.
James, P.D. (1972) *An Unsuitable Job for a Woman*, with *Death of an Expert Witness* and *Innocent Blood*, in *The P.D. James Omnibus*, London: Faber & Faber [1990].
—— (1982) *The Skull Beneath the Skin*, London: Faber & Faber.
—— (1986) *A Taste for Death*, London: Faber & Faber.
—— (1989) *Devices and Desires*, London: Faber & Faber.
Miner, Valerie (1982) *Murder in the English Department*, London: Women's Press.
O'Rourke, Rebecca (1987) *Jumping the Cracks*, London: Virago.
Slovo, Gillian (1984) *Morbid Symptoms*, London: Pluto Press.
—— (1986) *Death by Analysis*, London: Women's Press.
—— (1987) *Death Comes Staccato*, London: Women's Press.
Smith, Joan (1988) *A Masculine Ending*, London: Faber & Faber.
—— (1988) *Why Aren't They Screaming?*, London: Faber & Faber.
Wilson, Barbara (1984) *Murder in the Collective*, London: Women's Press.
—— (1987) *Sisters of the Road*, London: Women's Press.
Wilson, Barbara (1989) *The Dog Collar Murders*, London: Virago.

Wings, Mary (1986) *She Came Too Late*, London: Women's Press.
—— (1988) *She Came in a Flash*, London: Women's Press.
Zaremba, Eve (1987) *Beyond Hope*, London: Virago [1989].

BIBLIOGRAPHY AND REFERENCES

Adam, Ruth (1975) *A Woman's Place*, London: Chatto & Windus.

Auden, W.H. (1963) 'The Guilty Vicarage', in *The Dyer's Hand*, London: Faber & Faber.

Bargainnier, Earl F. (1981) *The Gentle Art of Murder*, Bowling Green, Ohio: Bowling Green State University Press.

Barnard, Robert (1980) *A Talent to Deceive: An Appreciation of Agatha Christie*, London: Collins.

Beauman, Nicola (1983) *A Very Great Profession: The Woman's Novel 1914–39*, London: Virago.

Binyon, T.J. (1989) *Murder Will Out: The Detective in Fiction*, Oxford: Oxford University Press.

Bott, Alan and Clephane, Irene (1932) *Our Mothers*, London: Gollancz.

Cawelti, John (1980) 'The Study of Literary Formulas', in Winks.

Chesterton, G.K. (1976) 'A Defence of Detective Stories' and 'The Detection Club Oath', in Haycraft.

Craig, Patricia and Cadogan, Mary (1986) *The Lady Investigates: Women Detectives and Spies in Fiction*, Oxford: Oxford University Press.

Daly, Mary (1979) *Gyn/Ecology*, London: Women's Press.

Dyhouse, Carol (1989) *Feminism and the Family in England, 1880–1939*, Oxford: Basil Blackwell.

Fitzgibbon, Russell, H. (1980) *The Agatha Christie Companion*, Bowling Green, Ohio: Bowling Green State University Press.

Green, Jan (ed.) (1989) *Reader, I Murdered Him: An Anthology of Original Crime Stories*, with an Introduction by Alison Hennegan, London: Women's Press.

Grella, George (1980) 'Murder and Manners: The Formal Detective Story', in Winks.

Haycraft, Howard (ed.) (1976) *The Art of the Mystery Story: A Collection of Critical Essays*, New York: Biblio and Tannen.

Heilbrun, Carolyn G. (1989) *Writing a Woman's Life*, London: Women's Press.

Hughes, M.V. (1977) *A London Child of the 1870s*, Oxford: Oxford University Press.

Jeffreys, Sheila (1985) *The Spinster and Her Enemies: Feminism and Sexuality 1880–1930*, London: Pandora Press.

Kaplan, Cora (1986) 'An Unsuitable Genre For a Feminist', *Women's Review* vol. 8, June.

Knight, Stephen (1980) *Form and Ideology in Crime Fiction*, London: Macmillan.

Knox, Ronald A. (1976) 'A Detective Story Decalogue', in Haycraft.

Leavis, Q.D. (1932) *Fiction and the Reading Public*, London: Chatto & Windus.

Maida, Patricia D. and Spornick, Nicholas B. (1982) *Murder She Wrote: A Study of Agatha Christie*, Bowling Green, Ohio: Bowling Green State University Press.

Mandel, Ernest (1983) *Delightful Murder: A Social History of the Crime Story*, London: Pluto Press.

Mann, Jessica (1981) *Deadlier Than the Male: An Investigation into Feminine Crime Writing*, London: David and Charles.

Morgan, Janet (1984) *Agatha Christie, A Biography*, London: Collins.

Osborne, Charles (1982) *The Life and Crimes of Agatha Christie*, London: Collins.

Sanders, Dennis and Lovallo, Len (1985) *The Agatha Christie Companion: The Complete Guide to Agatha Christie's Life and Work*, London: W.H. Allen.

Sayers, Dorothy L. (1980) 'Introduction to *The Omnibus of Crime* (first published 1928) in Winks.

Slung, Michele B. (ed.) (1976) *Crime on Her Mind: Fifteen Stories of Female Sleuths from the Victorian Era to the Forties*, London: Michael Joseph.

Symons, Julian (1972) *Bloody Murder. From the Detective Story to the Crime Novel: A History*, London: Faber & Faber.

Watson, Colin (1971) *Snobbery with Violence. Crime Stories and Their Audience*, London: Eyre & Spottiswoode.

Winks, Robin (ed.) (1980) *Detective Fiction: A Collection of Critical Essays*, New Jersey: Prentice-Hall.

Van Dine, S.S. (1976) 'Twenty Rules for Writing Detective Stories', in Haycraft.

Zahava, Irene (ed.) (1988) *The Womansleuth Anthology: Contemporary Mystery Stories by Women*, Freedom, CA: The Crossing Press.